DEPARTMENT OF THE TREASURY

TECHNICAL EXPLANATION OF

THE PROTOCOL DONE AT CHELSEA ON SEPTEMBER 21, 2007

AMENDING THE CONVENTION BETWEEN

THE UNITED STATES OF AMERICA AND CANADA

WITH RESPECT TO TAXES ON INCOME AND ON CAPITAL

DONE AT WASHINGTON ON SEPTEMBER 26, 1980,

AS AMENDED BY THE PROTOCOLS DONE ON

JUNE 14, 1983, MARCH 28, 1994, MARCH 17, 1995, AND JULY 29, 1997

DEPARTMENT OF THE TREASURY
TECHNICAL EXPLANATION OF
THE PROTOCOL DONE AT CHELSEA ON SEPTEMBER 21, 2007
AMENDING THE CONVENTION BETWEEN
THE UNITED STATES OF AMERICA AND CANADA
WITH RESPECT TO TAXES ON INCOME AND ON CAPITAL
DONE AT WASHINGTON ON SEPTEMBER 26, 1980,
AS AMENDED BY THE PROTOCOLS DONE ON
JUNE 14, 1983, MARCH 28, 1994, MARCH 17, 1995, AND JULY 29, 1997

INTRODUCTION

This is a Technical Explanation of the Protocol signed at Chelsea on September 21, 2007 (the "Protocol"), amending the Convention between the United States of America and Canada with Respect to Taxes on Income and on Capital done at Washington on September 26, 1980, as amended by the Protocols done on June 14, 1983, March 28, 1994, March 17, 1995, and July 29, 1997 (the "existing Convention"). The existing Convention as modified by the Protocol shall be referred to as the "Convention."

Negotiation of the Protocol took into account the U.S. Treasury Department's current tax treaty policy and the Treasury Department's Model Income Tax Convention, published on November 15, 2006 (the "U.S. Model"). Negotiations also took into account the Model Tax Convention on Income and on Capital, published by the Organisation for Economic Cooperation and Development (the "OECD Model"), and recent tax treaties concluded by both countries.

The Technical Explanation is an official United States guide to the Protocol. The Government of Canada has reviewed this document and subscribes to its contents. In the view of both governments, this document accurately reflects the policies behind particular Protocol provisions, as well as understandings reached with respect to the application and interpretation of the Protocol and the Convention.

References made to the "existing Convention" are intended to put various provisions of the Protocol into context. The Technical Explanation does not, however, provide a complete comparison between the provisions of the existing Convention and the amendments made by the Protocol. The Technical Explanation is not intended to provide a complete guide to the existing Convention as amended by the Protocol. To the extent that the existing Convention has not been amended by the Protocol, the prior technical explanations of the Convention remain the official explanations. References in this Technical Explanation to "he"' or "his" should be read to mean "he or she" or "his or her." References to the "Code" are to the Internal Revenue Code.

On the date of signing of the Protocol, the United States and Canada exchanged two sets of diplomatic notes. Each of these notes sets forth provisions and understandings related to the Protocol and the Convention, and comprises an integral part of the overall agreement between the United States and Canada. The first note, the

"Arbitration Note," relates to the implementation of new paragraphs 6 and 7 of Article XXVI (Mutual Agreement Procedure), which provide for binding arbitration of certain disputes between the competent authorities. The second note, the "General Note," relates more generally to issues of interpretation or application of various provisions of the Protocol.

Article 1

Article 1 of the Protocol adds subparagraph 1(k) to Article III (General Definitions) to address the definition of "national" of a Contracting State as used in the Convention. The Contracting States recognize that Canadian tax law does not draw distinctions based on nationality as such. Nevertheless, at the request of the United States, the definition was added and contains references to both citizenship and nationality. The definition includes any individual possessing the citizenship or nationality of a Contracting State and any legal person, partnership or association whose status is determined by reference to the laws in force in a Contracting State. The existing Convention contains one reference to the term "national" in paragraph 1 of Article XXVI (Mutual Agreement Procedure). The Protocol adds another reference in paragraph 1 of Article XXV (Non-Discrimination) to ensure that nationals of the United States are covered by the non-discrimination provisions of the Convention. The definition added by the Protocol is consistent with the definition provided in other U.S. tax treaties.

The General Note provides that for purposes of paragraph 2 of Article III, as regards the application at any time of the Convention, any term not defined in the Convention shall, unless the context otherwise requires or the competent authorities otherwise agree to a common meaning pursuant to Article XXVI (Mutual Agreement Procedure), have the meaning which it has at that time under the law of that State for the purposes of the taxes to which the Convention apply, any meaning under the applicable tax laws of that State prevailing over a meaning given to the term under other laws of that State.

Article 2

Article 2 of the Protocol replaces paragraph 3 of Article IV (Residence) of the existing Convention to address the treatment of so-called dual resident companies. Article 2 of the Protocol also adds new paragraphs 6 and 7 to Article IV to determine whether income is considered to be derived by a resident of a Contracting State when such income is derived through a fiscally transparent entity.

Paragraph 3 of Article IV – Dual resident companies

Paragraph 3, which addresses companies that are otherwise considered resident in each of the Contracting States, is replaced. The provisions of paragraph 3, and the date upon which these provisions are effective, are consistent with an understanding reached between the United States and Canada on September 18, 2000, to clarify the residence of a company under the Convention when the company has engaged in a so-called corporate "continuance" transaction. The paragraph applies only where, by reason of the rules set forth in paragraph 1 of Article IV (Residence), a company is a resident of both Contracting States.

Subparagraph 3(a) provides a rule to address the situation when a company is a resident of both Contracting States but is created under the laws in force in only one of the Contracting States. In such a case, the rule provides that the company is a resident only of the Contracting State under which it is created. For example, if a company is incorporated in the United States but the company is also otherwise considered a resident of Canada because the company is managed in Canada, subparagraph 3(a) provides that the company shall be considered a resident only of the United States for purposes of the Convention. Subparagraph 3(a) is intended to operate in a manner similar to the first sentence of former paragraph 3. However, subparagraph 3(a) clarifies that such a company must be considered created in only one of the Contracting States to fall within the scope of subparagraph 3(a). In some cases, a company may engage in a corporate continuance transaction and retain its charter in the Contracting State from which it continued, while also being considered as created in the State to which the company continued. In such cases, the provisions of subparagraph 3(a) shall not apply because the company would be considered created in both of the Contracting States.

Subparagraph 3(b) addresses all cases involving a dual resident company that are not addressed in subparagraph 3(a). Thus, subparagraph 3(b) applies to continuance transactions occurring between the Contracting States if, as a result, a company otherwise would be considered created under the laws of each Contracting State, *e.g.*, because the corporation retained its charter in the first State. Subparagraph 3(b) would also address so-called serial continuance transactions where, for example, a company continues from one of the Contracting States to a third country and then continues into the other Contracting State without having ceased to be treated as resident in the first Contracting State.

Subparagraph 3(b) provides that if a company is considered to be a resident of both Contracting States, and the residence of such company is not resolved by subparagraph 3(a), then the competent authorities of the Contracting States shall endeavor to settle the question of residency by a mutual agreement procedure and determine the mode of application of the Convention to such company. Subparagraph 3(b) also provides that in the absence of such agreement, the company shall not be considered a resident of either Contracting State for purposes of claiming any benefits under the Convention.

Paragraphs 6 and 7 of Article IV – income, profit, or gain derived through fiscally transparent entities

New paragraphs 6 and 7 are added to Article IV to provide specific rules for the treatment of amounts of income, profit or gain derived through or paid by fiscally transparent entities such as partnerships and certain trusts. Fiscally transparent entities, as explained more fully below, are in general entities the income of which is taxed at the beneficiary, member, or participant level. Entities that are subject to tax, but with respect to which tax may be relieved under an integrated system, are not considered fiscally transparent entities. Entities that are fiscally transparent for U.S. tax purposes include partnerships, common investment trusts under section 584, grantor trusts, and business entities such as a limited liability company ("LLC") that is treated as a partnership or is disregarded as an entity separate from its owner for U.S. tax purposes. Entities falling within this description in Canada are (except to the extent the law provides otherwise) partnerships and what are known as "bare" trusts.

United States tax law also considers a corporation that has made a valid election to be taxed under Subchapter S of Chapter 1 of the Internal Revenue Code (an "S corporation") to be fiscally transparent within the meaning explained below. Thus, if a U.S. resident derives income from Canada through an S corporation, the U.S. resident will under new paragraph 6 be considered for purposes of the Convention as the person who derived the income. Exceptionally, because Canada will ordinarily accept that an S corporation is itself resident in the United States for purposes of the Convention, Canada will allow benefits under the Convention to the S corporation in its own right. In a reverse case, however – that is, where the S corporation is owned by a resident of Canada and has U.S.-source income, profits or gains – the Canadian resident will not be considered as deriving the income by virtue of subparagraph 7 (a) as Canada does not see the S corporation as fiscally transparent.

Under both paragraph 6 and paragraph 7, it is relevant whether the treatment of an amount of income, profit or gain derived by a person through an entity under the tax law of the residence State is "the same as its treatment would be if that amount had been derived directly." For purposes of paragraphs 6 and 7, whether the treatment of an amount derived by a person through an entity under the tax law of the residence State is the same as its treatment would be if that amount had been derived directly by that person shall be determined in accordance with the principles set forth in Code section 894 and the regulations under that section concerning whether an entity will be treated as fiscally transparent with respect to an item of income received by the entity. Treas. Reg. section 1.894-1(d)(3)(iii) provides that an entity will be fiscally transparent under the laws of an interest holder's jurisdiction with respect to an item of income to the extent that the laws of that jurisdiction require the interest holder resident in that jurisdiction to separately take into account on a current basis the interest holder's respective share of the item of income paid to the entity, whether or not distributed to the interest holder, and the character and source of the item in the hands of the interest holder are determined as if such item were realized directly from the source from which realized by the entity. Although Canada does not have analogous provisions in its domestic law, it is anticipated that principles comparable to those described above will apply.

Paragraph 6

Under paragraph 6, an amount of income, profit or gain is considered to be derived by a resident of a Contracting State (residence State) if 1) the amount is derived by that person through an entity (other than an entity that is a resident of the other Contracting State (source State), and 2) by reason of that entity being considered fiscally transparent under the laws of the residence State, the treatment of the amount under the tax law of the residence State is the same as its treatment would be if that amount had been derived directly by that person. These two requirements are set forth in subparagraphs 6(a) and 6(b), respectively.

For example, if a U.S. resident owns a French entity that earns Canadian-source dividends and the entity is considered fiscally transparent under U.S. tax law, the U.S. resident is considered to derive the Canadian-source dividends for purposes of Article IV (and thus, the dividends are considered as being "paid to" the resident) because the U.S. resident is considered under the tax law of the United States to have derived the dividend through the French entity and, because the entity is treated as fiscally transparent under U.S. tax law, the treatment of the income under U.S. tax law is the same as its treatment would be if that amount had been derived directly by the U.S. resident. This result obtains even if the French entity is viewed differently under the tax laws of Canada or of France (*i.e.*, the French entity is treated under Canadian law or under French tax law as not fiscally transparent).

Similarly, if a Canadian resident derives U.S.-source income, profit or gain through an entity created under Canadian law that is considered a partnership for Canadian tax purposes but a corporation for U.S. tax purposes, U.S.-source income, profit or gain derived through such entity by the Canadian resident will be considered to be derived by the Canadian resident in considering the application of the Convention.

Application of paragraph 6 and related treaty provisions by Canada

In determining the entitlement of a resident of the United States to the benefits of the Convention, Canada shall apply the Convention within its own legal framework.

For example, assume that from the perspective of Canadian law an amount of income is seen as being paid from a source in Canada to USLLC, an entity that is entirely owned by U.S. persons and is fiscally transparent for U.S. tax purposes, but that Canada considers a corporation and, thus, under Canadian law, a taxpayer in its own right. Since USLLC is not itself taxable in the United States, it is not considered to be a U.S. resident under the Convention; but for new paragraph 6 Canada would not apply the Convention in taxing the income.

If new paragraph 6 applies in respect of an amount of income, profit or gain, such amount is considered as having been derived by one or more U.S. resident shareholders of USLLC, and Canada shall grant benefits of the Convention to the payment to USLLC and eliminate or reduce Canadian tax as provided in the Convention. The effect of the rule is to suppress Canadian taxation of USLLC to give effect to the benefits available under the Convention to the U.S. residents in respect of the particular amount of income, profit or gain.

However, for Canadian tax purposes, USLLC remains the only "visible" taxpayer in relation to this amount. In other words, the Canadian tax treatment of this taxpayer (USLLC) is modified because of the entitlement of its U.S. resident shareholders to benefits under the Convention, but this does not alter USLLC's status under Canadian law. Canada does not, for example, treat USLLC as though it did not exist, substituting the shareholders for it in the role of taxpayer under Canada's system.

Some of the implications of this are as follows. First, Canada will not require the shareholders of USLLC to file Canadian tax returns in respect of income that benefits from new paragraph 6. Instead, USLLC itself will file a Canadian tax return in which it will claim the benefit of the paragraph and supply any documentation required to support the claim. (The Canada Revenue Agency will supply additional practical guidance in this regard, including instructions for seeking to establish entitlement to Convention benefits in advance of payment.) Second, as is explained in greater detail below, if the income in question is business profits, it will be necessary to determine whether the income was earned through a permanent establishment in Canada. This determination will be based on the presence and activities in Canada of USLLC itself, not of its shareholders acting in their own right.

Determination of the existence of a permanent establishment from the business activities of a fiscally transparent entity

New paragraph 6 applies not only in respect of amounts of dividends, interest and royalties, but also profit (business income), gains and other income. It may thus be relevant in cases where a resident of one Contracting State carries on business in the other State through an entity that has a different characterization in each of the two Contracting States.

Application of new paragraph 6 and the provisions of Article V (Permanent Establishment) by Canada

Assume, for instance, that a resident of the United States is part owner of a U.S. limited liability company (USLLC) that is treated in the United States as a fiscally transparent entity, but in Canada as a corporation. Assume one of the other two shareholders of USLLC is resident in a country that does not have a tax treaty with Canada and that the remaining shareholder is resident in a country with which Canada does have a tax treaty, but that the treaty does not include a provision analogous to paragraph 6.

Assume further that USLLC carries on business in Canada, but does not do so through a permanent establishment there. (Note that from the Canadian perspective, the presence or absence of a permanent establishment is evaluated with respect to USLLC only, which Canada sees as a potentially taxable entity in its own right.) Regarding Canada's application of the provisions of the Convention, the portion of USLLC's profits that belongs to the U.S. resident shareholder will not be taxable in Canada, provided that the U.S. resident meets the Convention's limitation on benefits provisions. Under paragraph 6, that portion is seen as having been derived by the U.S. resident shareholder, who is entitled to rely on Article VII (Business Profits). The balance of USLLC's profits will, however, remain taxable in Canada. Since USLLC is not itself resident in the United States for purposes of the Convention, in respect of that portion of its profits that is not considered to have been derived by a U.S. resident (or a resident of another country whose treaty with Canada includes a rule comparable to paragraph 6) it is not relevant whether or not it has a permanent establishment in Canada.

Another example would be the situation where a USLLC that is wholly owned by a resident of the U.S. carries on business in Canada through a permanent establishment. If the USLLC is fiscally transparent for U.S. tax purposes (and therefore, the conditions for the application of paragraph 6 are satisfied) then the USLLC's profits will be treated as having been derived by its U.S. resident owner inclusive of all attributes of that income (*e.g.*, such as having been earned through a permanent establishment). However, since the USLLC remains the only "visible" taxpayer for Canadian tax purposes, it is the USLLC, and not the U.S. shareholder, that is subject to tax on the profits that are attributable to the permanent establishment.

Application of new paragraph 6 and the provisions of Article V (Permanent Establishment) by the United States

It should be noted that in the situation where a person is considered to derive income through an entity, the United States looks in addition to such person's activities in order to determine whether he has a permanent establishment. Assume that a Canadian resident and a resident in a country that does not have a tax treaty with the United States are owners of CanLP. Assume further that Can LP is an entity that is considered fiscally transparent for Canadian tax purposes but is not considered fiscally transparent for U.S. tax purposes, and that CanLP carries on business in the United States. If CanLP carries on the business through a permanent establishment, that permanent establishment may be attributed to the partners. Moreover, in determining whether there is a permanent establishment, the activities of both the entity and its partners will be considered. If CanLP does not carry on the business through a permanent establishment, the Canadian resident, who derives income through the partnership, may claim the benefits of Article VII (Business Profits) of the Convention with respect to such income, assuming that the income is not otherwise attributable to a permanent establishment of the partner. In any case, the third country partner cannot claim the benefits of Article VII of the Convention between the United States and Canada.

Paragraph 7

Paragraph 7 addresses situations where an item of income, profit or gain is considered not to be paid to or derived by a person who is a resident of a Contracting State. The paragraph is divided into two subparagraphs.

Under subparagraph 7(a), an amount of income, profit or gain is considered not to be paid to or derived by a person who is a resident of a Contracting State (the residence State) if (1) the other Contracting State (the source State) views the person as deriving the amount through an entity that is not a resident of the residence State, and (2) by reason of the entity not being treated as fiscally transparent under the laws of the residence State, the treatment of the amount under the tax law of the residence State is not the same as its treatment would be if that amount had been derived directly by the person.

For example, assume USCo, a company resident in the United States, is a part owner of CanLP, an entity that is considered fiscally transparent for Canadian tax purposes, but is not considered fiscally transparent for U.S. tax purposes. CanLP receives a dividend from a Canadian company in which it owns stock. Under Canadian tax law USCo is viewed as deriving a Canadian-source dividend through CanLP. For U.S. tax purposes, CanLP, and not USCo, is viewed as deriving the dividend. Because the treatment of the dividend under U.S. tax law in this case is not the same as the treatment under U.S. law if USCo derived the dividend directly, subparagraph 7(a) provides that USCo will not be considered as having derived the dividend. The result would be the same if CanLP were a third-country entity that was viewed by the United States as not fiscally transparent, but was viewed by Canada as fiscally transparent. Similarly, income from U.S. sources received by an entity organized under the laws of the United States that is treated for Canadian tax purposes as a corporation and is owned by shareholders who are residents of Canada is not considered derived by the shareholders of that U.S. entity even if, under U.S. tax law, the entity is treated as fiscally transparent.

Subparagraph 7(b) provides that an amount of income, profit or gain is not considered to be paid to or derived by a person who is a resident of a Contracting State (the residence State) where the person is considered under the tax law of the other Contracting State (the source State) to have received the amount from an entity that is a resident of that other State (the source State), but by reason of the entity being treated as fiscally transparent under the laws of the Contracting State of which the person is resident (the residence State), the treatment of such amount under the tax law of that State (the residence State) is not the same as the treatment would be if that entity were not treated as fiscally transparent under the laws of that State (the residence State).

That is, under subparagraph 7(b), an amount of income, profit or gain is not considered to be paid to or derived by a resident of a Contracting State (the residence State) if: (1) the other Contracting State (the source State) views such person as receiving the amount from an entity resident in the source State; (2) the entity is viewed as fiscally transparent under the laws of the residence State; and (3) by reason of the entity being treated as fiscally transparent under the laws of the residence State, the treatment of the amount received by that person under the tax law of the residence State is not the same as its treatment would be if the entity were not treated as fiscally transparent under the laws of the residence State.

For example, assume that USCo, a company resident in the United States is the sole owner of CanCo, an entity that is considered under Canadian tax law to be a corporation that is resident in Canada but is considered under U.S. tax law to be disregarded as an entity separate from its owner. Assume further that USCo is considered under Canadian tax law to have received a dividend from CanCo.

In such a case, Canada, the source State, views USCo as receiving income (*i.e.*, a dividend) from a corporation that is a resident of Canada (CanCo), CanCo is viewed as fiscally transparent under the laws of the United States, the residence State, and by reason of CanCo being disregarded under U.S. tax law, the treatment under U.S. tax law of the payment is not the same as its treatment would be if the entity were regarded as a corporation under U.S. tax law. That is, the payment is disregarded for U.S. tax purposes, whereas if U.S. tax law regarded CanCo as a corporation, the payment would be treated as a dividend. Therefore, subparagraph 7(b) would apply to provide that the income is not considered to be paid to or derived by USCo.

The same result obtains if, in the above example, USCo is considered under Canadian tax law to have received an interest or royalty payment (instead of a dividend) from CanCo. Under U.S. law, because CanCo is disregarded as an entity separate from its owner, the payment is disregarded, whereas if CanCo were treated as not fiscally transparent, the payment would be treated as interest or a royalty, as the case may be. Therefore, subparagraph 7(b) would apply to provide that such amount is not considered to be paid to or derived by USCo.

The application of subparagraph 7(b) differs if, in the above example, USCo (as well as other persons) are owners of CanCo, a Canadian entity that is considered under Canadian tax law to be a corporation that is resident in Canada but is considered under U.S. tax law to be a partnership (as opposed to being disregarded). Assume that USCo is considered under Canadian tax law to have received a dividend from CanCo. Such payment is viewed under Canadian tax law as a dividend, but under U.S. tax law is viewed as a partnership distribution. In such a case, Canada views USCo as receiving income (*i.e.*, a dividend) from an entity that is a resident of Canada (CanCo), CanCo is viewed as fiscally transparent under the laws of the United States, the residence State, and by reason of CanCo being treated as a partnership under U.S. tax law, the treatment under U.S. tax law of the payment (as a partnership distribution) is not the same as the treatment would be if CanCo were not fiscally transparent under U.S. tax law (as a dividend). As a result, subparagraph 7(b) would apply to provide that such amount is not considered paid to or derived by the U.S. resident.

As another example, assume that CanCo, a company resident in Canada, is the owner of USLP, an entity that is considered under U.S. tax law (by virtue of an election) to be a corporation resident in the United States, but that is considered under Canadian tax law to be a branch of CanCo. Assume further that CanCo is considered under U.S. tax law to have received a dividend from USLP. In this case, the United States views CanCo as receiving income (*i.e.*, a dividend) from an entity that is resident in the United States (USLP), but by reason of USLP being a branch under Canadian tax law, the treatment under Canadian tax law of the payment is not the same as its treatment would be if USLP were a company under Canadian tax law. That is, the payment is treated as a branch remittance for Canadian tax purposes, whereas if Canadian tax law regarded USLP as a corporation, the payment would be treated as a dividend. Therefore, subparagraph 7(b) would apply to provide that the income is not considered to be paid to or derived by CanCo. The same result would obtain in the case of interest or royalties paid by USLP to CanCo.

Paragraphs 6 and 7 apply to determine whether an amount is considered to be derived by (or paid to) a person who is a resident of Canada or the United States. If, as a result of paragraph 7, a person is not considered to have derived or received an amount of income, profit or gain, that person shall not be entitled to the benefits of the Convention with respect to such amount. Additionally, for purposes of application of the Convention by the United States, the treatment of such payments under Code section 894(c) and the regulations thereunder would not be relevant.

New paragraphs 6 and 7 are not an exception to the saving clause of paragraph 2 of Article XXIX (Miscellaneous Rules). Accordingly, subparagraph 7(b) does not prevent a Contracting State from taxing an entity that is treated as a resident of that State under its tax law. For example, if a U.S. partnership with members who are residents of Canada elects to be taxed as a corporation for U.S. tax purposes, the United States will tax that partnership on its worldwide income on a net basis, even if Canada views the partnership as fiscally transparent.

Interaction of paragraphs 6 and 7 with the determination of "beneficial ownership"

With respect to payments of income, profits or gain arising in a Contracting State and derived directly by a resident of the other Contracting State (and not through a fiscally transparent entity), the term "beneficial owner" is defined under the internal law of the country imposing tax (*i.e.*, the source State). Thus, if the payment arising in a Contracting State is derived by a resident of the other State who under the laws of the first-mentioned State is determined to be a nominee or agent acting on behalf of a person that is not a resident of that other State, the payment will not be entitled to the benefits of the Convention. However, payments arising in a Contracting State and derived by a nominee on behalf of a resident of that other State would be entitled to benefits. These limitations are confirmed by paragraph 12 of the Commentary to Article 10 of the OECD Model.

Special rules apply in the case of income, profits or gains derived through a fiscally transparent entity, as described in new paragraph 6 of Article IV. Residence State principles determine who derives the income, profits or gains, to assure that the income, profits or gains for which the source State grants benefits of the Convention will be taken into account for tax purposes by a resident of the residence State. Source country principles of beneficial ownership apply to determine whether the person who derives the income, profits or gains, or another resident of the other Contracting State, is the beneficial owner of the income, profits or gains. The source State may conclude that the person who derives the income, profits or gains in the residence State is a mere nominee, agent, conduit, etc., for a third country resident and deny benefits of the Convention. If the person who derives the income, profits or gains under paragraph 6 of Article IV would not be treated under the source State's principles for determining beneficial ownership as a nominee, agent, custodian, conduit, etc., that person will be treated as the beneficial owner of the income, profits or gains for purposes of the Convention.

Assume, for instance, that interest arising in the United States is paid to CanLP, an entity established in Canada which is treated as fiscally transparent for Canadian tax purposes but is treated as a company for U.S. tax purposes. CanCo, a company incorporated in Canada, is the sole interest holder in CanLP. Paragraph 6 of Article IV provides that CanCo derives the interest. However, if under the laws of the United States regarding payments to nominees, agents, custodians and conduits, CanCo is found be a nominee, agent, custodian or conduit for a person who is not a resident of Canada, CanCo will not be considered the beneficial owner of the interest and will not be entitled to the benefits of Article XI with respect to such interest. The payment may be entitled to benefits, however, if CanCo is found to be a nominee, agent, custodian or conduit for a person who is a resident of Canada.

With respect to Canadian-source income, profit or gains, beneficial ownership is to be determined under Canadian law. For example, assume that LLC, an entity that is treated as fiscally transparent for U.S. tax purposes, but as a corporation for Canadian tax purposes, is owned by USCo, a U.S. resident company. LLC receives Canadian-source income. The question of the beneficial ownership of the income received by LLC is determined under Canadian law. If LLC is considered the beneficial owner of the income under Canadian law, paragraph 6 shall apply to extend benefits of the Convention to the income received by LLC to the extent that the Canadian-source income is derived by U.S. resident members of LLC.

Article 3

Article 3 of the Protocol amends Article V (Permanent Establishment) of the Convention. Paragraph 1 of Article 3 of the Protocol adds a reference in Paragraph 6 of Article IV to new paragraph 9 of Article V. Paragraph 2 of Article 3 of the Protocol sets forth new paragraphs 9 and 10 of Article V.

Paragraph 9 of Article V

New paragraph 9 provides a special rule (subject to the provisions of paragraph 3) for an enterprise of a Contracting State that provides services in the other Contracting State, but that does not have a permanent establishment by virtue of the preceding paragraphs of the Article. If (and only if) such an enterprise meets either of two tests as provided in subparagraphs 9(a) and 9(b), the enterprise will be deemed to provide those services through a permanent establishment in the other State.

The first test as provided in subparagraph 9(a) has two parts. First, the services must be performed in the other State by an individual who is present in that other State for a period or periods aggregating 183 days or more in any twelve-month period. Second, during that period or periods, more than 50 percent of the gross active business revenues of the enterprise (including revenue from active business activities unrelated to the provision of services) must consist of income derived from the services performed in that State by that individual. If the enterprise meets both of these tests, the enterprise will be deemed to provide the services through a permanent establishment. This test is employed to determine whether an enterprise is deemed to have a permanent establishment by virtue of the presence of a single individual (*i.e.*, a natural person).

For the purposes of subparagraph 9(a), the term "gross active business revenues" shall mean the gross revenues attributable to active business activities that the enterprise has charged or should charge for its active business activities, regardless of when the actual billing will occur or of domestic law rules concerning when such revenues should be taken into account for tax purposes. Such active business activities are not restricted to the activities related to the provision of services. However, the term does not include income from passive investment activities.

As an example of the application of subparagraph 9(a), assume that Mr. X, an individual resident in the United States, is one of the two shareholders and employees of USCo, a company resident in the United States that provides engineering services. During the 12-month period beginning December 20 of Year 1 and ending December 19 of Year 2, Mr. X is present in Canada for periods totaling 190 days, and during those periods, 70 percent of all of the gross active business revenues of USCo attributable to business activities are derived from the services that Mr. X performs in Canada. Because both of the criteria of subparagraph 9(a) are satisfied, USCo will be deemed to have a permanent establishment in Canada by virtue of that subparagraph.

The second test as provided in subparagraph 9(b) provides that an enterprise will have a permanent establishment if the services are provided in the other State for an aggregate of 183 days or more in any twelve-month period with respect to the same or connected projects for customers who either are residents of the other State or maintain a permanent establishment in the other State with respect to which the services are provided. The various conditions that have to be satisfied in order for subparagraph 9(b) to have application are described in detail below.

In addition to meeting the 183-day threshold, the services must be provided for customers who either are residents of the other State or maintain a permanent establishment in that State. The intent of this requirement is to reinforce the concept that unless there is a customer in the other State, such enterprise will not be deemed as participating sufficiently in the economic life of that other State to warrant being deemed to have a permanent establishment.

Assume for example, that CanCo, a Canadian company, wishes to acquire USCo, a company in the United States. In preparation for the acquisition, CanCo hires Canlaw, a Canadian law firm, to conduct a due diligence evaluation of USCo's legal and financial standing in the United States. Canlaw sends a staff attorney to the United States to perform the due diligence analysis of USCo. That attorney is present and working in the United States for greater than 183 days. If the remuneration paid to Canlaw for the attorney's services does not constitute more than 50 percent of Canlaw's gross active business revenues for the period during which the attorney is present in the United States, Canlaw will not be deemed to provide the services through a permanent establishment in the United States by virtue of subparagraph 9(a). Additionally, because the services are being provided for a customer (CanCo) who neither is a resident of the United States nor maintains a permanent establishment in the United States to which the services are provided, Canlaw will also not have a permanent establishment in the United States by virtue of subparagraph 9(b).

Paragraph 9 applies only to the provision of services, and only to services provided by an enterprise to third parties. Thus, the provision does not have the effect of deeming an enterprise to have a permanent establishment merely because services are provided to that enterprise. Paragraph 9 only applies to services that are performed or provided by an enterprise of a Contracting State within the other Contracting State. It is therefore not sufficient that the relevant services be merely furnished to a resident of the other Contracting State. Where, for example, an enterprise provides customer support or other services by telephone or computer to customers located in the other State, those would not be covered by paragraph 9 because they are not performed or provided by that enterprise within the other State. Another example would be that of an architect who is hired to design blueprints for the construction of a building in the other State. As part of completing the project, the architect must make site visits to that other State, and his days of presence there would be counted for purposes of determining whether the 183-day threshold is satisfied. However, the days that the architect spends working on the blueprint in his home office shall not count for purposes of the 183-day threshold, because the architect is not performing or providing those services within the other State.

For purposes of determining whether the time threshold has been met, subparagraph 9(b) permits the aggregation of services that are provided with respect to connected projects. Paragraph 2 of the General Note provides that for purposes of subparagraph 9(b), projects shall be considered to be connected if they constitute a coherent whole, commercially and geographically. The determination of whether projects are connected should be determined from the point of view of the enterprise (not that of the customer), and will depend on the facts and circumstances of each case. In determining the existence of commercial coherence, factors that would be relevant include: 1) whether the projects would, in the absence of tax planning considerations, have been concluded pursuant to a single contract; 2) whether the nature of the work involved under different projects is the same; and 3) whether the same individuals are providing the services under the different projects. Whether the work provided is covered by one or multiple contracts may be relevant, but not determinative, in finding that projects are commercially coherent.

The aggregation rule addresses, for example, potentially abusive situations in which work has been artificially divided into separate components in order to avoid meeting the 183-day threshold. Assume for example, that a technology consultant has been hired to install a new computer system for a company in the other country. The work will take ten months to complete. However, the consultant purports to divide the work into two five-month projects with the intention of circumventing the rule in subparagraph 9(b). In such case, even if the two projects were considered separate, they will be considered to be commercially coherent. Accordingly, subject to the additional requirement of geographic coherence, the two projects could be considered to be connected, and could therefore be aggregated for purposes of subparagraph 9(b). In contrast, assume that the technology consultant is contracted to install a particular computer system for a company, and is also hired by that same company, pursuant to a separate contract, to train its employees on the use of another computer software that is unrelated to the first system. In this second case, even though the contracts are both concluded between the same two parties, there is no commercial coherence to the two projects, and the time spent fulfilling the two contracts may not be aggregated for purposes of subparagraph 9(b). Another example of projects that do not have commercial coherence would be the case of a law firm which, as one project provides tax advice to a customer from one portion of its staff, and as another project provides trade advice from another portion of its staff, both to the same customer.

Additionally, projects, in order to be considered connected, must also constitute a geographic whole. An example of projects that lack geographic coherence would be a case in which a consultant is hired to execute separate auditing projects at different branches of a bank located in different cities pursuant to a single contract. In such an example, while the consultant's projects are commercially coherent, they are not geographically coherent and accordingly the services provided in the various branches shall not be aggregated for purposes of applying subparagraph 9(b). The services provided in each branch should be considered separately for purposes of subparagraph 9(b).

The method of counting days for purposes of subparagraph 9(a) differs slightly from the method for subparagraph 9(b). Subparagraph 9(a) refers to days in which an individual is present in the other country. Accordingly, physical presence during a day is sufficient. In contrast, subparagraph 9(b) refers to days during which services are provided by the enterprise in the other country. Accordingly, non-working days such as weekends or holidays would not count for purposes of subparagraph 9(b), as long as no services are actually being provided while in the other country on those days. For the purposes of both subparagraphs, even if the enterprise sends many individuals simultaneously to the other country to provide services, their collective presence during one calendar day will count for only one day of the enterprise's presence in the other country. For instance, if an enterprise sends 20 employees to the other country to provide services to a client in the other country for 10 days, the enterprise will be considered present in the other country only for 10 days, not 200 days (20 employees x 10 days).

By deeming the enterprise to provide services through a permanent establishment in the other Contracting State, paragraph 9 allows the application of Article VII (Business Profits), and accordingly, the taxation of the services shall be on a net-basis. Such taxation is also limited to the profits attributable to the activities carried on in performing the relevant services. It will be important to ensure that only the profits properly attributable to the functions performed and risks assumed by provision of the services will be attributed to the deemed permanent establishment.

In addition to new paragraph 9, Article 3 of the Protocol amends paragraph 6 of Article V of the Convention to include a reference to paragraph 9. Therefore, in no case will paragraph 9 apply to deem services to be provided through a permanent establishment if the services are limited to those mentioned in paragraph 6 which, if performed through a fixed place of business, would not make the fixed place of business a permanent establishment under the provisions of that paragraph.

The competent authorities are encouraged to consider adopting rules to reduce the potential for excess withholding or estimated tax payments with respect to employee wages that may result from the application of this paragraph. Further, because paragraph 6 of Article V applies notwithstanding paragraph 9, days spent on preparatory or auxiliary activities shall not be taken into account for purposes of applying subparagraph 9(b).

Paragraph 10 of Article V

Paragraph 2 of Article 3 of the Protocol also sets forth new paragraph 10 of Article V. The provisions of new paragraph 10 are identical to paragraph 9 of Article V as it existed prior to the Protocol. New paragraph 10 provides that the provisions of Article V shall be applied in determining whether any person has a permanent establishment in any State.

Article 4

Article 4 of the Protocol replaces paragraph 2 of Article VII (Business Profits).

New paragraph 2 provides that where a resident of either Canada or the United States carries on (or has carried on) business in the other Contracting State through a permanent establishment in that other State, both Canada and the United States shall attribute to permanent establishments in their respective states those business profits which the permanent establishment might be expected to make if it were a distinct and separate person engaged in the same or similar activities under the same or similar conditions and dealing wholly independently with the resident and with any other person related to the resident. The term "related to the resident" is to be interpreted in accordance with paragraph 2 of Article IX (Related Persons). The reference to other related persons is intended to make clear that the test of paragraph 2 is not restricted to independence between a permanent establishment and a home office.

New paragraph 2 is substantially similar to paragraph 2 as it existed before the Protocol. However, in addition to the reference to a resident of a Contracting State who "carries on" business in the other Contracting State, the Protocol incorporates into the Convention the rule of Code section 864(c)(6) by adding "or has carried on" to address circumstances where, as a result of timing, income may be attributable to a permanent establishment that no longer exists in one of the Contracting States. In such cases, the income is properly within the scope of Article VII. Conforming changes are also made in the Protocol to Articles X (Dividends), XI (Interest), and XII (Royalties) of the Convention where Article VII would apply. As is explained in paragraph 5 of the General Note, these revisions to the Convention are only intended to clarify the application of the existing provisions of the Convention.

The following example illustrates the application of paragraph 2. Assume a company that is a resident of Canada and that maintains a permanent establishment in the United States winds up the permanent establishment's business and sells the permanent establishment's inventory and assets to a U.S. buyer at the end of year 1 in exchange for an installment obligation payable in full at the end of year 3. Despite the fact that the company has no permanent establishment in the United States in year 3, the United States may tax the deferred income payment recognized by the company in year 3.

The "attributable to" concept of paragraph 2 provides an alternative to the analogous but somewhat different "effectively connected" concept in Code section 864(c). Depending on the circumstances, the amount of income "attributable to" a permanent establishment under Article VII may be greater or less than the amount of income that would be treated as "effectively connected" to a U.S. trade or business under Code section 864. In particular, in the case of financial institutions, the use of internal dealings to allocate income within an enterprise may produce results under Article VII that are significantly different than the results under the effectively connected income rules. For example, income from interbranch notional principal contracts may be taken into account under Article VII, notwithstanding that such transactions may be ignored for purposes of U.S. domestic law. A taxpayer may use the treaty to reduce its taxable income, but may not use both treaty and Code rules where doing so would thwart the intent of either set of rules. *See* Rev. Rul. 84-17, 1984-1 C.B. 308.

The profits attributable to a permanent establishment may be from sources within or without a Contracting State. However, as stated in the General Note, the business profits attributable to a permanent establishment include only those profits derived from the assets used, risks assumed, and activities performed by the permanent establishment.

The language of paragraph 2, when combined with paragraph 3 dealing with the allowance of deductions for expenses incurred for the purposes of earning the profits, incorporates the arm's length standard for purposes of determining the profits attributable to a permanent establishment. The United States and Canada generally interpret the arm's length standard in a manner consistent with the OECD Transfer Pricing Guidelines.

Paragraph 9 of the General Note confirms that the arm's length method of paragraphs 2 and 3 consists of applying the OECD Transfer Pricing Guidelines, but taking into account the different economic and legal circumstances of a single legal entity (as opposed to separate but associated enterprises). Thus, any of the methods used in the Transfer Pricing Guidelines, including profits methods, may be used as appropriate and in accordance with the Transfer Pricing Guidelines. However, the use of the Transfer Pricing Guidelines applies only for purposes of attributing profits within the legal entity. It does not create legal obligations or other tax consequences that would result from transactions having independent legal significance. Thus, the Contracting States agree that the notional payments used to compute the profits that are attributable to a permanent establishment will not be taxed as if they were actual payments for purposes of other taxing provisions of the Convention, for example, for purposes of taxing a notional royalty under Article XII (Royalties).

One example of the different circumstances of a single legal entity is that an entity that operates through branches rather than separate subsidiaries generally will have lower capital requirements because all of the assets of the entity are available to support all of the entity's liabilities (with some exceptions attributable to local regulatory restrictions). This is the reason that most commercial banks and some insurance companies operate through branches rather than subsidiaries. The benefit that comes from such lower capital costs must be allocated among the branches in an appropriate manner. This issue does not arise in the case of an enterprise that operates through separate entities, since each entity will have to be separately capitalized or will have to compensate another entity for providing capital (usually through a guarantee).

Under U.S. domestic regulations, internal "transactions" generally are not recognized because they do not have legal significance. In contrast, the rule provided by the General Note is that such internal dealings may be used to attribute income to a permanent establishment in cases where the dealings accurately reflect the allocation of risk within the enterprise. One example is that of global trading in securities. In many cases, banks use internal swap transactions to transfer risk from one branch to a central location where traders have the expertise to manage that particular type of risk. Under paragraph 2 as set forth in the Protocol, such a bank may also use such swap transactions as a means of attributing income between the branches, if use of that method is the "best method" within the meaning of regulation section 1.482-1(c). The books of a branch will not be respected, however, when the results are inconsistent with a functional analysis. So, for example, income from a transaction that is booked in a particular branch (or home office) will not be treated as attributable to that location if the sales and risk management functions that generate the income are performed in another location.

The understanding in the General Note also affects the interpretation of paragraph 3 of Article VII. Paragraph 3 provides that in determining the business profits of a permanent establishment, deductions shall be allowed for the expenses incurred for the purposes of the permanent establishment, ensuring that business profits will be taxed on a net basis. This rule is not limited to expenses incurred exclusively for the purposes of the permanent establishment, but includes expenses incurred for the purposes of the enterprise as a whole, or that part of the enterprise that includes the permanent establishment. Deductions are to be allowed regardless of which accounting unit of the enterprise books the expenses, so long as they are incurred for the purposes of the permanent establishment. For example, a portion of the interest expense recorded on the books of the home office in one State may be deducted by a permanent establishment in the other. The amount of the expense that must be allowed as a deduction is determined by applying the arm's length principle.

As noted above, paragraph 9 of the General Note provides that the OECD Transfer Pricing Guidelines apply, by analogy, in determining the profits attributable to a permanent establishment. Accordingly, a permanent establishment may deduct payments made to its head office or another branch in compensation for services performed for the benefit of the branch. The method to be used in calculating that amount will depend on the terms of the arrangements between the branches and head office. For example, the enterprise could have a policy, expressed in writing, under which each business unit could use the services of lawyers employed by the head office. At the end of each year, the costs of employing the lawyers would be charged to each business unit according to the amount of services used by that business unit during the year. Since this has the characteristics of a cost-sharing arrangement and the allocation of costs is based on the benefits received by each business unit, such a cost allocation would be an acceptable

15

means of determining a permanent establishment's deduction for legal expenses. Alternatively, the head office could agree to employ lawyers at its own risk, and to charge an arm's length price for legal services performed for a particular business unit. If the lawyers were under-utilized, and the "fees" received from the business units were less than the cost of employing the lawyers, then the head office would bear the excess cost. If the "fees" exceeded the cost of employing the lawyers, then the head office would keep the excess to compensate it for assuming the risk of employing the lawyers. If the enterprise acted in accordance with this agreement, this method would be an acceptable alternative method for calculating a permanent establishment's deduction for legal expenses.

The General Note also makes clear that a permanent establishment cannot be funded entirely with debt, but must have sufficient capital to carry on its activities as if it were a distinct and separate enterprise. To the extent that the permanent establishment has not been attributed capital for profit attribution purposes, a Contracting State may attribute such capital to the permanent establishment, in accordance with the arm's length principle, and deny an interest deduction to the extent necessary to reflect that capital attribution. The method prescribed by U.S. domestic law for making this attribution is found in Treas. Reg. section 1.882-5. Both section 1.882-5 and the method prescribed in the General Note start from the premise that all of the capital of the enterprise supports all of the assets and risks of the enterprise, and therefore the entire capital of the enterprise must be allocated to its various businesses and offices.

However, section 1.882-5 does not take into account the fact that some assets create more risk for the enterprise than do other assets. An independent enterprise would need less capital to support a perfectly-hedged U.S. Treasury security than it would need to support an equity security or other asset with significant market and/or credit risk. Accordingly, in some cases section 1.882-5 would require a taxpayer to allocate more capital to the United States, and therefore would reduce the taxpayer's interest deduction more, than is appropriate. To address these cases, the General Note allows a taxpayer to apply a more flexible approach that takes into account the relative risk of its assets in the various jurisdictions in which it does business. In particular, in the case of financial institutions other than insurance companies, the amount of capital attributable to a permanent establishment is determined by allocating the institution's total equity between its various offices on the basis of the proportion of the financial institution's risk-weighted assets attributable to each of them. This recognizes the fact that financial institutions are in many cases required to risk-weight their assets for regulatory purposes and, in other cases, will do so for business reasons even if not required to do so by regulators. However, risk-weighting is more complicated than the method prescribed by section 1.882-5. Accordingly, to ease this administrative burden, taxpayers may choose to apply the principles of Treas. Reg. section 1.882-5(c) to determine the amount of capital allocable to its U.S. permanent establishment, in lieu of determining its allocable capital under the risk-weighted capital allocation method provided by the General Note, even if it has otherwise chosen the principles of Article VII rather than the effectively connected income rules of U.S. domestic law. It is understood that this election is not binding for purposes of Canadian taxation unless the result is in accordance with the arm's length principle.

As noted in the Convention, nothing in paragraph 3 requires a Contracting State to allow the deduction of any expenditure which, by reason of its nature, is not generally allowed as a deduction under the tax laws in that State.

Article 5

Article 5 makes a number of amendments to Article X (Dividends) of the existing Convention. As with other benefits of the Convention, the benefits of Article X are available to a resident of a Contracting State only if that resident is entitled to those benefits under the provisions of Article XXIX A (Limitation on Benefits).

See the Technical Explanation for new paragraphs 6 and 7 of Article IV (Residence) for discussion regarding the interaction between domestic law concepts of beneficial ownership and the treaty rules to determine when a person is considered to derive an item of income for purposes of obtaining benefits of the Convention such as withholding rate reductions.

Paragraph 1

Paragraph 1 of Article 5 of the Protocol replaces subparagraph 2(a) of Article X of the Convention. In general, paragraph 2 limits the amount of tax that may be imposed on dividends by the Contracting State in which the company paying the dividends is resident if the beneficial owner of the dividends is a resident of the other Contracting State. Subparagraph 2(a) limits the rate to 5 percent of the gross amount of the dividends if the beneficial owner is a company that owns 10 percent or more of the voting stock of the company paying the dividends.

The Protocol adds a parenthetical to address the determination of the requisite ownership set forth in subparagraph 2(a) when the beneficial owner of dividends receives the dividends through an entity that is considered fiscally transparent in the beneficial owner's Contracting State. The added parenthetical stipulates that voting stock in a company paying the dividends that is indirectly held through an entity that is considered fiscally transparent in the beneficial owner's Contracting State is taken into account, provided the entity is not a resident of the other Contracting State. The United States views the new parenthetical as merely a clarification.

For example, assume USCo, a U.S. corporation, directly owns 2 percent of the voting stock of CanCo, a Canadian company that is considered a corporation in the United States and Canada. Further, assume that USCo owns 18 percent of the interests in LLC, an entity that in turn owns 50 percent of the voting stock of CanCo. CanCo pays a dividend to each of its shareholders. Provided that LLC is fiscally transparent in the United States and not considered a resident of Canada, USCo's 9 percent ownership in CanCo through LLC (50 percent x 18 percent) is taken into account in determining whether USCo meets the 10 percent ownership threshold set forth in subparagraph 2(a). In this example, USCo may aggregate its voting stock interests in CanCo that it owns directly and through LLC to determine if it satisfies the ownership requirement of subparagraph 2(a). Accordingly, USCo will be entitled to the 5 percent rate of withholding on dividends paid with respect to both its voting stock held through LLC and its voting stock held directly. Alternatively, if, for example, all of the shareholders of LLC were natural persons, the 5 percent rate would not apply.

Paragraph 2

Paragraph 2 of Article 5 of the Protocol replaces the definition of the term "dividends" provided in paragraph 3 of Article X of the Convention. The new definition conforms to the U.S. Model formulation. Paragraph 3 defines the term dividends broadly and flexibly. The definition is intended to cover all arrangements that yield a return on

17

an equity investment in a corporation as determined under the tax law of the source State, as well as arrangements that might be developed in the future.

The term dividends includes income from shares, or other corporate rights that are not treated as debt under the law of the source State, that participate in the profits of the company. The term also includes income that is subjected to the same tax treatment as income from shares by the law of the source State. Thus, for example, a constructive dividend that results from a non-arm's length transaction between a corporation and a related party is a dividend. In the case of the United States the term "dividend" includes amounts treated as a dividend under U.S. law upon the sale or redemption of shares or upon a transfer of shares in a reorganization. *See, e.g.*, Rev. Rul. 92-85, 1992-2 C.B. 69 (sale of foreign subsidiary's stock to U.S. sister company is a deemed dividend to extent of the subsidiary's and sister company's earnings and profits). Further, a distribution from a U.S. publicly traded limited partnership that is taxed as a corporation under U.S. law is a dividend for purposes of Article X. However, a distribution by a limited liability company is not considered by the United States to be a dividend for purposes of Article X, provided the limited liability company is not characterized as an association taxable as a corporation under U.S. law.

Paragraph 3 of the General Note states that distributions from Canadian income trusts and royalty trusts that are treated as dividends as a result of changes to Canada's taxation of income and royalty trusts enacted in 2007 (S.C. 2007, c. 29) shall be treated as dividends for the purposes of Article X.

Additionally, a payment denominated as interest that is made by a thinly capitalized corporation may be treated as a dividend to the extent that the debt is recharacterized as equity under the laws of the source State. At the time the Protocol was signed, interest payments subject to Canada's thin-capitalization rules were not recharacterized as dividends.

Paragraph 3

Paragraph 3 of Article 5 of the Protocol replaces paragraph 4 of Article X. New paragraph 4 is substantially similar to paragraph 4 as it existed prior to the Protocol. New paragraph 4, however, adds clarifying language consistent with the changes made in Articles 4, 6, and 7 of the Protocol with respect to income attributable to a permanent establishment that has ceased to exist. Paragraph 4 provides that the limitations of paragraph 2 do not apply if the beneficial owner of the dividends carries on or has carried on business in the State in which the company paying the dividends is a resident through a permanent establishment situated there, and the stockholding in respect of which the dividends are paid is effectively connected to such permanent establishment. In such a case, the dividends are taxable pursuant to the provisions of Article VII (Business Profits). Thus, dividends paid in respect of holdings forming part of the assets of a permanent establishment or which are otherwise effectively connected to such permanent establishment will be taxed on a net basis using the rates and rules of taxation generally applicable to residents of the State in which the permanent establishment is situated.

To conform with Article 9 of the Protocol, which deletes Article XIV (Independent Personal Services) of the Convention, paragraph 4 of Article 5 of the Protocol also amends paragraph 5 of Article X by omitting the reference to a "fixed base."

Paragraph 4

To conform with Article 9 of the Protocol, which deletes Article XIV (Independent Personal Services) of the Convention, paragraph 4 of Article 5 of the Protocol amends paragraph 5 of Article X by omitting the reference to a "fixed base."

Paragraph 5

Paragraph 5 of Article 5 of the Protocol replaces subparagraph 7(c) of Article X of the existing Convention. Consistent with current U.S. tax treaty policy, new subparagraph 7(c) provides rules that expand the application of subparagraph 2(b) for the treatment of dividends paid by a Real Estate Investment Trust (REIT). New subparagraph 7(c) maintains the rule of the existing Convention that dividends paid by a REIT are not eligible for the 5 percent maximum rate of withholding tax of subparagraph 2(a), and provides that the 15 percent maximum rate of withholding tax of subparagraph 2(b) applies to dividends paid by REITs only if one of three conditions is met.

First, the dividend will qualify for the 15 percent maximum rate if the beneficial owner of the dividend is an individual holding an interest of not more than 10 percent in the REIT. For this purpose, subparagraph 7(c) also provides that where an estate or testamentary trust acquired its interest in a REIT as a consequence of the death of an individual, the estate or trust will be treated as an individual for the five-year period following the death. Thus, dividends paid to an estate or testamentary trust in respect of a holding of less than a 10 percent interest in the REIT also will be entitled to the 15 percent rate of withholding, but only for up to five years after the death.

Second, the dividend will qualify for the 15 percent maximum rate if it is paid with respect to a class of stock that is publicly traded and the beneficial owner of the dividend is a person holding an interest of not more than 5 percent of any class of the REIT's stock.

Third, the dividend will qualify for the 15 percent maximum rate if the beneficial owner of the dividend holds an interest in the REIT of 10 percent or less and the REIT is "diversified." A REIT is diversified if the gross value of no single interest in real property held by the REIT exceeds 10 percent of the gross value of the REIT's total interest in real property. For purposes of this diversification test, foreclosure property is not considered an interest in real property, and a REIT holding a partnership interest is treated as owning its proportionate share of any interest in real property held by the partnership.

A resident of Canada directly holding U.S. real property would pay U.S. tax either at a 30 percent rate of withholding tax on the gross income or at graduated rates on the net income. By placing the real property in a REIT, the investor absent a special rule could transform real estate income into dividend income, taxable at the rates provided in Article X, significantly reducing the U.S. tax that otherwise would be imposed. Subparagraph 7(c) prevents this result and thereby avoids a disparity between the taxation of direct real estate investments and real estate investments made through REIT conduits. In the cases in which subparagraph 7(c) allows a dividend from a REIT to be eligible for the 15 percent maximum rate of withholding tax, the holding in the REIT is not considered the equivalent of a direct holding in the underlying real property.

Article 6

Article 6 of the Protocol replaces Article XI (Interest) of the existing Convention. Article XI specifies the taxing jurisdictions over interest income of the States of source and residence and defines the terms necessary to apply Article XI. As with other benefits of the Convention, the benefits of Article XI are available to a resident of a Contracting State only if that resident is entitled to those benefits under the provisions of Article XXIX A (Limitation on Benefits).

Paragraph 1 of Article XI

New paragraph 1 generally grants to the residence State the exclusive right to tax interest beneficially owned by its residents and arising in the other Contracting State. See the Technical Explanation for new paragraphs 6 and 7 of Article IV (Residence) for discussion regarding the interaction between domestic law concepts of beneficial ownership and the treaty rules to determine when a person is considered to derive an item of income for purposes of obtaining benefits under the Convention such as withholding rate reductions.

Subparagraph 3(d) of Article 27 of the Protocol provides an additional rule regarding the application of paragraph 1 during the first two years that end after the Protocol's entry into force. This rule is described in detail in the Technical Explanation to Article 27.

Paragraph 2 of Article XI

Paragraph 2 of new Article XI is substantially identical to paragraph 4 of Article XI of the existing Convention.

Paragraph 2 defines the term "interest" as used in Article XI to include, *inter alia*, income from debt claims of every kind, whether or not secured by a mortgage. Interest that is paid or accrued subject to a contingency is within the ambit of Article XI. This includes income from a debt obligation carrying the right to participate in profits. The term does not, however, include amounts that are treated as dividends under Article X (Dividends).

The term "interest" also includes amounts subject to the same tax treatment as income from money lent under the law of the State in which the income arises. Thus, for purposes of the Convention, amounts that the United States will treat as interest include (i) the difference between the issue price and the stated redemption price at maturity of a debt instrument (*i.e.*, original issue discount (OID)), which may be wholly or partially realized on the disposition of a debt instrument (section 1273), (ii) amounts that are imputed interest on a deferred sales contract (section 483), (iii) amounts treated as interest or OID under the stripped bond rules (section 1286), (iv) amounts treated as original issue discount under the below-market interest rate rules (section 7872), (v) a partner's distributive share of a partnership's interest income (section 702), (vi) the interest portion of periodic payments made under a "finance lease" or similar contractual arrangement that in substance is a borrowing by the nominal lessee to finance the acquisition of property, (vii) amounts included in the income of a holder of a residual interest in a real estate mortgage investment conduit (REMIC) (section 860E), because these amounts generally are subject to the same taxation treatment as interest under U.S. tax law, and (viii) interest with respect to notional principal contracts that are re-characterized as loans because of a "substantial non-periodic payment."

Paragraph 3 of Article XI

Paragraph 3 is in all material respects the same as paragraph 5 of Article XI of the existing Convention. New paragraph 3 adds clarifying language consistent with the changes made in Articles 4, 5, and 7 of the Protocol with respect to income attributable to a permanent establishment that has ceased to exist. Also, consistent with the changes described in Article 9 of the Protocol, discussed below, paragraph 3 does not contain references to the performance of independent personal services through a fixed base.

Paragraph 3 provides an exception to the exclusive residence taxation rule of paragraph 1 in cases where the beneficial owner of the interest carries on business through a permanent establishment in the State of source and the interest is effectively connected to that permanent establishment. In such cases the provisions of Article VII (Business Profits) will apply and the source State will retain the right to impose tax on such interest income.

Paragraph 4 of Article XI

Paragraph 4 is in all material respects the same as paragraph 6 of Article XI of the existing Convention. The only difference is that, consistent with the changes described below with respect to Article 9 of the Protocol, paragraph 4 does not contain references to a fixed base.

Paragraph 4 establishes the source of interest for purposes of Article XI. Interest is considered to arise in a Contracting State if the payer is that State, or a political subdivision, local authority, or resident of that State. However, in cases where the person paying the interest, whether a resident of a Contracting State or of a third State, has in a State other than that of which he is a resident a permanent establishment in connection with which the indebtedness on which the interest was paid was incurred, and such interest is borne by the permanent establishment, then such interest is deemed to arise in the State in which the permanent establishment is situated and not in the State of the payer's residence. Furthermore, pursuant to paragraphs 1 and 4, and Article XXII (Other Income), Canadian tax will not be imposed on interest paid to a U.S. resident by a company resident in Canada if the indebtedness is incurred in connection with, and the interest is borne by, a permanent establishment of the company situated in a third State. For the purposes of this Article, "borne by" means allowable as a deduction in computing taxable income.

Paragraph 5 of Article XI

Paragraph 5 is identical to paragraph 7 of Article XI of the existing Convention.

Paragraph 5 provides that in cases involving special relationships between the payer and the beneficial owner of interest income or between both of them and some other person, Article XI applies only to that portion of the total interest payments that would have been made absent such special relationships (*i.e.*, an arm's-length interest payment). Any excess amount of interest paid remains taxable according to the laws of the United States and Canada, respectively, with due regard to the other provisions of the Convention.

Paragraph 6 of Article XI

New paragraph 6 provides anti-abuse exceptions to exclusive residence State taxation in paragraph 1 for two classes of interest payments.

The first class of interest, dealt with in subparagraphs 6(a) and 6(b), is so-called "contingent interest." With respect to interest arising in the United States, subparagraph 6(a) refers to contingent interest of a type that does not qualify as portfolio interest under U.S. domestic law. The cross-reference to the U.S. definition of contingent interest, which is found in Code section 871(h)(4), is intended to ensure that the exceptions of Code section 871(h)(4)(C) will apply. With respect to Canada, such interest is defined in subparagraph 6(b) as any interest arising in Canada that is determined by reference to the receipts, sales, income, profits or other cash flow of the debtor or a related person, to any change in the value of any property of the debtor or a related person or to any dividend, partnership distribution or similar payment made by the debtor or a related person.[1] Any such interest may be taxed in Canada according to the laws of Canada.

Under subparagraph 6(a) or 6(b), if the beneficial owner is a resident of the other Contracting State, the gross amount of the "contingent interest" may be taxed at a rate not exceeding 15 percent.

The second class of interest is dealt with in subparagraph 6(c). This exception is consistent with the policy of Code sections 860E(e) and 860G(b) that excess inclusions with respect to a real estate mortgage investment conduit (REMIC) should bear full U.S. tax in all cases. Without a full tax at source, foreign purchasers of residual interests would have a competitive advantage over U.S. purchasers at the time these interests are initially offered. Also, absent this rule, the U.S. fisc would suffer a revenue loss with respect to mortgages held in a REMIC because of opportunities for tax avoidance created by differences in the timing of taxable and economic income produced by these interests.

Therefore, subparagraph 6(c) provides a bilateral provision that interest that is an excess inclusion with respect to a residual interest in a REMIC may be taxed by each State in accordance with its domestic law. While the provision is written reciprocally, at the time the Protocol was signed, the provision had no application in respect of Canadian-source interest, as Canada did not have REMICs.

Paragraph 7 of Article XI

Paragraph 7 is in all material respects the same as paragraph 8 of Article XI of the existing Convention. The only difference is that, consistent with the changes made in Article 9 of the Protocol, paragraph 7 removes the references to a fixed base.

Paragraph 7 restricts the right of a Contracting State to impose tax on interest paid by a resident of the other Contracting State. The first State may not impose any tax on such interest except insofar as the interest is paid to a resident of that State or arises in that State or the debt claim in respect of which the interest is paid is effectively connected with a permanent establishment situated in that State.

---

[1] New subparagraph 6(b) of Article XI erroneously refers to a "similar payment made by the debtor to a related person." The correct formulation, which the Contracting States agree to apply, is "similar payment made by the debtor or a related person."

Relationship to other Articles

Notwithstanding the foregoing limitations on source State taxation of interest, the saving clause of paragraph 2 of Article XXIX (Miscellaneous Rules) permits the United States to tax its residents and citizens, subject to the special foreign tax credit rules of paragraph 5 of Article XXIV (Elimination of Double Taxation), as if the Convention had not come into force.

Article 7

Article 7 of the Protocol amends Article XII (Royalties) of the existing Convention. As with other benefits of the Convention, the benefits of Article XII are available to a resident of a Contracting State only if that resident is entitled to those benefits under the provisions of Article XXIX A (Limitation on Benefits).

See the Technical Explanation for new paragraphs 6 and 7 of Article IV (Residence) for discussion regarding the interaction between domestic law concepts of beneficial ownership and the treaty rules to determine when a person is considered to derive an item of income for purposes of obtaining benefits of the Convention such as withholding rate reductions.

Paragraph 1

Paragraph 1 of Article 7 of the Protocol replaces paragraph 5 of Article XII of the Convention. In all material respects, new paragraph 5 is the same as paragraph 5 of Article XII of the existing Convention. However, new paragraph 5 adds clarifying language consistent with the changes made in Articles 4, 5, and 6 of the Protocol with respect to income attributable to a permanent establishment that has ceased to exist. To conform with Article 9 of the Protocol, which deletes Article XIV (Independent Personal Services) of the Convention, paragraph 1 of Article 7 of the Protocol also amends paragraph 5 of Article XII by omitting the reference to a "fixed base."

New paragraph 5 provides that the 10 percent limitation on tax in the source State provided by paragraph 2, and the exemption in the source State for certain royalties provided by paragraph 3, do not apply if the beneficial owner of the royalties carries on or has carried on business in the source State through a permanent establishment and the right or property in respect of which the royalties are paid is attributable to such permanent establishment. In such case, the royalty income would be taxable by the source State under the provisions of Article VII (Business Profits).

Paragraph 2

Paragraph 2 of Article 7 of the Protocol sets forth a new subparagraph 6(a) of Article XII that is in all material respects the same as subparagraph 6(a) of Article XII of the existing Convention. The only difference is that, consistent with the changes made in Article 9 of the Protocol, new subparagraph 6(a) omits references to a "fixed base."

Paragraph 3

Paragraph 3 of Article 7 of Protocol amends paragraph 8 of Article XII of the Convention to remove references to a "fixed base." In addition, paragraph 8 of the General Note confirms the intent of the Contracting States that the reference in subparagraph 3(c) of Article XII of the Convention to information provided in connection with a franchise agreement generally refers only to information that governs or otherwise deals with the operation (whether by the payer or by another person) of the franchise, and not to other information concerning industrial, commercial or scientific experience that is held for resale or license.

Article 8

Paragraph 1

Paragraph 1 of Article 8 of the Protocol replaces paragraph 2 of Article XIII (Gains) of the existing Convention. Consistent with Article 9 of the Protocol, new paragraph 2 does not contain any reference to property pertaining to a fixed base or to the performance of independent personal services.

New paragraph 2 of Article XIII provides that the Contracting State in which a resident of the other Contracting State has or had a permanent establishment may tax gains from the alienation of personal property constituting business property if such gains are attributable to such permanent establishment. Unlike paragraph 1 of Article VII (Business Profits), paragraph 2 limits the right of the source State to tax such gains to a twelve-month period following the termination of the permanent establishment.

Paragraph 2

Paragraph 2 of Article 8 of the Protocol replaces paragraph 5 of Article XIII of the existing Convention. In general, new paragraph 5 provides an exception to the general rule stated in paragraph 4 that gains from the alienation of any property, other than property referred to in paragraphs 1, 2, and 3, shall be taxable only in the Contracting State of which the alienator is a resident. Paragraph 5 provides that a Contracting State may, according to its domestic law, impose tax on gains derived by an individual who is a resident of the other Contracting State if such individual was a resident of the first-mentioned State for 120 months (whether or not consecutive) during any period of 20 consecutive years preceding the alienation of the property, and was a resident of that State at any time during the 10-year period immediately preceding the alienation of the property. Further, the property (or property received in substitution in a tax-free transaction in the first-mentioned State) must have been owned by the individual at the time he ceased to be a resident of the first-mentioned State and must not have been property that the individual was treated as having alienated by reason of ceasing to be a resident of the first-mentioned State and becoming a resident of the other Contracting State.

The provisions of new paragraph 5 are substantially similar to paragraph 5 of Article XIII of the existing Convention. However, the Protocol adds a new requirement to paragraph 5 that the property not be "a property that the individual was treated as having alienated by reason of ceasing to be a resident of the first-mentioned State and becoming a resident of the other Contracting State." This new requirement reflects the fact that the main purpose of paragraph 5 – ensuring that gains that accrue while an individual is resident in a Contracting State remain taxable for the stated time after the individual has moved to the other State – is met if that pre-departure gain is taxed in the first State immediately before the individual's emigration. This rule applies whether or not the individual makes the election provided by paragraph 7 of Article XIII, as amended, which is described below.

Paragraph 3

Paragraph 3 of Article 8 of the Protocol replaces paragraph 7 of Article XIII.

24

The purpose of paragraph 7, in both its former and revised form, is to provide a rule to coordinate U.S. and Canadian taxation of gains in the case of a timing mismatch. Such a mismatch may occur, for example, where a Canadian resident is deemed, for Canadian tax purposes, to recognize capital gain upon emigrating from Canada to the United States, or in the case of a gift that Canada deems to be an income producing event for its tax purposes but with respect to which the United States defers taxation while assigning the donor's basis to the donee. The former paragraph 7 resolved the timing mismatch of taxable events by allowing the individual to elect to be liable to tax in the deferring Contracting State as if he had sold and repurchased the property for an amount equal to its fair market value at a time immediately prior to the deemed alienation.

The election under former paragraph 7 was not available to certain non-U.S. citizens subject to tax in Canada by virtue of a deemed alienation because such individuals could not elect to be liable to tax in the United States. To address this problem, the Protocol replaces the election provided in former paragraph 7, with an election by the taxpayer to be treated by a Contracting State as having sold and repurchased the property for its fair market value immediately before the taxable event in the other Contracting State. The election in new paragraph 7 therefore will be available to any individual who emigrates from Canada to the United States, without regard to whether the person is a U.S. citizen immediately before ceasing to be a resident of Canada. If the individual is not subject to U.S. tax at that time, the effect of the election will be to give the individual an adjusted basis for U.S. tax purposes equal to the fair market value of the property as of the date of the deemed alienation in Canada, with the result that only post-emigration gain will be subject to U.S. tax when there is an actual alienation. If the Canadian resident is also a U.S. citizen at the time of his emigration from Canada, then the provisions of new paragraph 7 would allow the U.S. citizen to accelerate the tax under U.S. tax law and allow tax credits to be used to avoid double taxation. This would also be the case if the person, while not a U.S. citizen, would otherwise be subject to taxation in the United States on a disposition of the property.

In the case of Canadian taxation of appreciated property given as a gift, absent paragraph 7, the donor could be subject to tax in Canada upon making the gift, and the donee may be subject to tax in the United States upon a later disposition of the property on all or a portion of the same gain in the property without the availability of any foreign tax credit for the tax paid to Canada. Under new paragraph 7, the election will be available to any individual who pays taxes in Canada on a gain arising from the individual's gifting of a property, without regard to whether the person is a U.S. taxpayer at the time of the gift. The effect of the election in such case will be to give the donee an adjusted basis for U.S. tax purposes equal to the fair market value as of the date of the gift. If the donor is a U.S. taxpayer, the effect of the election will be the realization of gain or loss for U.S. purposes immediately before the gift. The acceleration of the U.S. tax liability by reason of the election in such case enables the donor to utilize foreign tax credits and avoid double taxation with respect to the disposition of the property.

Generally, the rule does not apply in the case of death. Note, however, that Article XXIX B (Taxes Imposed by Reason of Death) of the Convention provides rules that coordinate the income tax that Canada imposes by reason of death with the U.S. estate tax.

If in one Contracting State there are losses and gains from deemed alienations of different properties, then paragraph 7 must be applied consistently in the other Contracting State within the taxable period with respect to all such properties. Paragraph 7 only applies, however, if the deemed alienations of the properties result in a net gain.

Taxpayers may make the election provided by new paragraph 7 only with respect to property that is subject to a Contracting State's deemed disposition rules and with respect to which gain on a deemed alienation is recognized for that Contracting State's tax purposes in the taxable year of the deemed alienation. At the time the Protocol was signed, the following were the main types of property that were excluded from the deemed disposition rules in the case of individuals (including trusts) who cease to be residents of Canada: real property situated in Canada; interests and rights in respect of pensions; life insurance policies (other than segregated fund (investment) policies); rights in respect of annuities; interests in testamentary trusts, unless acquired for consideration; employee stock options; property used in a business carried on through a permanent establishment in Canada (including intangibles and inventory); interests in most Canadian personal trusts; Canadian resource property; and timber resource property.

Paragraph 4

Consistent with the provisions of Article 9 of the Protocol, paragraph 4 of Article 8 of the Protocol amends subparagraph 9(c) of Article XIII of the existing Convention to remove the words "or pertained to a fixed base."

Relationship to other Articles

The changes to Article XIII set forth in paragraph 3 were announced in a press release issued by the Treasury Department on September 18, 2000. Consistent with that press release, subparagraph 3(e) of Article 27 of the Protocol provides that the changes, jointly effectuated by paragraphs 2 and 3, will be generally effective for alienations of property that occur after September 17, 2000.

Article 9

To conform with the current U.S. and OECD Model Conventions, Article 9 of the Protocol deletes Article XIV (Independent Personal Services) of the Convention. The subsequent articles of the Convention are not renumbered. Paragraph 4 of the General Note elaborates that current tax treaty practice omits separate articles for independent personal services because a determination of the existence of a fixed base is qualitatively the same as the determination of the existence of a permanent establishment. Accordingly, the taxation of income from independent personal services is adequately governed by the provisions of Articles V (Permanent Establishment) and VII (Business Profits).

Article 10

Article 10 of the Protocol renames Article XV of the Convention as "Income from Employment" to conform with the current U.S. and OECD Model Conventions, and replaces paragraphs 1 and 2 of that renamed article consistent with the OECD Model Convention.

Paragraph 1

New paragraph 1 of Article XV provides that, in general, salaries, wages, and other remuneration derived by a resident of a Contracting State in respect of an employment are taxable only in that State unless the employment is exercised in the other Contracting State. If the employment is exercised in the other Contracting State, the entire remuneration derived therefrom may be taxed in that other State, subject to the provisions of paragraph 2.

New paragraph 1 of Article XV does not contain a reference to "similar" remuneration. This change was intended to clarify that Article XV applies to any form of compensation for employment, including payments in kind. This interpretation is consistent with paragraph 2.1 of the Commentary to Article 15 (Income from Employment) of the OECD Model and the Technical Explanation of the 2006 U.S. Model.

Paragraph 2

New paragraph 2 of Article XV provides two limitations on the right of a source State to tax remuneration for services rendered in that State. New paragraph 2 is divided into two subparagraphs that each sets forth a rule which, notwithstanding any contrary result due to the application of paragraph 1 of Article XV, prevents the source State from taxing income from employment in that State.

First, subparagraph 2(a) provides a safe harbor rule that the remuneration may not be taxed in the source State if such remuneration is $10,000 or less in the currency of the source State. This rule is identical to the rule in subparagraph 2(a) of Article XV of the existing Convention. It is understood that, consistent with the prior rule, the safe harbor will apply on a calendar-year basis.

Second, if the remuneration is not exempt from tax in the source State by virtue of subparagraph 2(a), subparagraph 2(b) provides an additional rule that the source State may not tax remuneration for services rendered in that State if the recipient is present in the source State for a period (or periods) that does not exceed in the aggregate 183 days in any twelve-month period commencing or ending in the fiscal year concerned, and the remuneration is not paid by or on behalf of a person who is a resident of that other State or borne by a permanent establishment in that other State. For purposes of this article, "borne by" means allowable as a deduction in computing taxable income.

Assume, for example, that Mr. X, an individual resident in Canada, is an employee of the Canadian permanent establishment of USCo, a U.S. company. Mr. X is sent to the United States to perform services and is present in the United States for less than 183 days. Mr. X receives more than $10,000 (U.S.) in the calendar year(s) in question. The remuneration paid to Mr. X for such services is not exempt from U.S. tax under paragraph 1, because his employer, USCo, is a resident of the United States and pays his remuneration. If instead Mr. X received less than $10,000 (U.S.), such earnings would be exempt from tax in the United States, because in all cases where an employee earns less than $10,000 in the currency of the source State, such earnings are exempt from tax in the source State.

As another example, assume Ms. Y, an individual resident in the United States is employed by USCo, a U.S. company. Ms. Y is sent to Canada to provide services in the Canadian permanent establishment of USCo. Ms. Y is present in Canada for less than 183 days. Ms. Y receives more than $10,000 (Canadian) in the calendar year(s) in question. USCo charges the Canadian permanent establishment for Ms. Y's remuneration, which the permanent establishment takes as a deduction in computing its taxable income. The remuneration paid to Ms. Y for such services is not exempt from Canadian tax under paragraph 1, because her remuneration is borne by the Canadian permanent establishment.

New subparagraph 2(b) refers to remuneration that is paid by or on behalf of a "person" who is a resident of the other Contracting State, as opposed to an "employer." This change is intended only to clarify that both the United States and Canada understand that in certain abusive cases, substance over form principles may be applied to recharacterize an employment relationship, as prescribed in paragraph 8 of the Commentary to Article 15 (Income from Employment) of the OECD Model. Subparagraph 2(b) is intended to have the same meaning as the analogous provisions in the U.S. and OECD Models.

Paragraph 6 of the General Note

Paragraph 6 of the General Note contains special rules regarding employee stock options. There are no similar rules in the U.S. Model or the OECD Model, although the issue is discussed in detail in paragraph 12 of the Commentary to Article 15 (Income from Employment) of the OECD Model.

The General Note sets forth principles that apply for purposes of applying Article XV and Article XXIV (Elimination of Double Taxation) to income of an individual in connection with the exercise or other disposal (including a deemed exercise or disposal) of an option that was granted to the individual as an employee of a corporation or mutual fund trust to acquire shares or units ("securities") of the employer in respect of services rendered or to be rendered by such individual, or in connection with the disposal (including a deemed disposal) of a security acquired under such an option. For this purpose, the term "employer" is considered to include any entity related to the service recipient. The reference to a disposal (or deemed disposal) reflects the fact that under Canadian law and under certain provisions of U.S. law, income or gain attributable to the granting or exercising of the option may, in some cases, not be recognized until disposition of the securities.

Subparagraph 6(a) of the General Note provides a specific rule to address situations where, under the domestic law of the Contracting States, an employee would be taxable by both Contracting States in respect of the income in connection with the exercise or disposal of the option. The rule provides an allocation of taxing rights where (1) an employee has been granted a stock option in the course of employment in one of the Contracting States, and (2) his principal place of employment has been situated in one or both of the Contracting States during the period between grant and exercise (or disposal) of the option. In this situation, each Contracting State may tax as Contracting State of source only that proportion of the income that relates to the period or periods between the grant and the exercise (or disposal) of the option during which the individual's principal place of employment was situated in that Contracting State. The proportion attributable to a Contracting State is determined by multiplying the income by a fraction, the numerator of which is the number of days between the grant and exercise (or disposal) of the option during which the employee's principal place of employment was situated in that Contracting State and the denominator of which is the total number of days between grant and exercise (or disposal) of the option that the employee was employed by the employer.

If the individual is a resident of one of the Contracting States at the time he exercises the option, that Contracting State will have the right, as the State of residence, to tax all of the income under the first sentence of paragraph 1 of Article XV. However, to the extent that the employee renders his employment in the other Contracting State for some period of time between the date of the grant of the option and the date of the exercise (or disposal) of the option, the proportion of the income that is allocated to the other Contracting State under subparagraph 6(a) of the General Note will, subject to paragraph 2, be taxable by that other State under the second sentence of paragraph 1 of Article XV of the Convention. For this purpose, the tests of paragraph 2 of Article XV are applied to the year or years in which the relevant services were performed in the other Contracting State (and not to the year in which the option is exercised or disposed). To the extent the same income is subject to taxation in both Contracting States after application of Article XV, double taxation will be alleviated under the rules of Article XXIV (Elimination of Double Taxation).

Subparagraph 6(b) of the General Note provides that notwithstanding subparagraph 6(a), if the competent authorities of both Contracting States agree that the terms of the option were such that the grant of the option is appropriately treated as transfer of ownership of the securities (*e.g.*, because the options were in-the-money or not subject to a substantial vesting period), then they may agree to attribute income accordingly.

Article 11

Consistent with Article 9 and paragraph 1 of Article 10 of the Protocol, paragraphs 1, 2, and 3 of Article 11 of the Protocol revise paragraphs 1, 2, and 4 of Article XVI (Artistes and Athletes) of the existing Convention by deleting references to former Article XIV (Independent Personal Services) of the Convention and deleting and replacing other language in acknowledgement of the renaming of Article XV (Income from Employment).

Article 12

Article 12 of the Protocol deletes Article XVII (Withholding of Taxes in Respect of Personal Services) from the Convention. However, the subsequent Articles are not renumbered.

Article 13

Article 13 of the Protocol replaces paragraphs 3, 4, and 7 and adds paragraphs 8 through 17 to Article XVIII (Pensions and Annuities) of the Convention.

Paragraph 1

Roth IRAs

Paragraph 1 of Article 13 of the Protocol separates the provisions of paragraph 3 of Article XVIII into two subparagraphs. Subparagraph 3(a) contains the existing definition of the term "pensions," while subparagraph 3(b) adds a new rule to address the treatment of Roth IRAs or similar plan (as described below).

Subparagraph 3(a) of Article XVIII provides that the term "pensions" for purposes of the Convention includes any payment under a superannuation, pension, or other retirement arrangement, Armed-Forces retirement pay, war veterans pensions and allowances, and amounts paid under a sickness, accident, or disability plan, but does not include payments under an income-averaging annuity contract (which are subject to Article XXII (Other Income)) or social security benefits, including social security benefits in respect of government services (which are subject to paragraph 5 of Article XVIII). Thus, the term "pensions" includes pensions paid by private employers (including pre-tax and Roth 401(k) arrangements) as well as any pension paid in respect of government services. Further, the definition of "pensions" includes, for example, payments from individual retirement accounts (IRAs) in the United States and from registered retirement savings plans (RRSPs) and registered retirement income funds (RRIFs) in Canada.

Subparagraph 3(b) of Article XVIII provides that the term "pensions" generally includes a Roth IRA, within the meaning of Code section 408A (or a similar plan described below). Consequently, under paragraph 1 of Article XVIII, distributions from a Roth IRA to a resident of Canada generally continue to be exempt from Canadian tax to the extent they would have been exempt from U.S. tax if paid to a resident of the United States. In addition, residents of Canada generally may make an election under paragraph 7 of Article XVIII to defer any taxation in Canada with respect to income accrued in a Roth IRA but not distributed by the Roth IRA, until such time as and to the extent that a distribution is made from the Roth IRA or any plan substituted therefore. Because distributions will be exempt from Canadian tax to the extent they would have been exempt from U.S. tax if paid to a resident of the United States, the effect of these rules is that, in most cases, no portion of the Roth IRA will be subject to taxation in Canada.

However, subparagraph 3(b) also provides that if an individual who is a resident of Canada makes contributions to his or her Roth IRA while a resident of Canada, other than rollover contributions from another Roth IRA (or a similar plan described below), the Roth IRA will cease to be considered a pension at that time with respect to contributions and accretions from such time and accretions from such time will be subject to tax in Canada in the year of accrual. Thus, the Roth IRA will in effect be bifurcated into a "frozen" pension that continues to be subject to the rules of Article XVIII and a savings account that is not subject to the rules of Article XVIII. It is understood by the Contracting States that, following a rollover contribution from a Roth 401(k) arrangement to a Roth IRA, the Roth IRA will continue to be treated as a pension subject to the rules of Article XVIII.

Assume, for example, that Mr. X moves to Canada on July 1, 2008. Mr. X has a Roth IRA with a balance of 1,100 on July 1, 2008. Mr. X elects under paragraph 7 of Article XVIII to defer any taxation in Canada with respect to income accrued in his Roth IRA while he is a resident of Canada. Mr. X makes no additional contributions to his Roth IRA until July 1, 2010, when he makes an after-tax contribution of 100. There are accretions of 20 during the period July 1, 2008 through June 30, 2010, which are not taxed in Canada by reason of the election under paragraph 7 of Article XVIII. There are additional accretions of 50 during the period July 1, 2010 through June 30, 2015, which are subject to tax in Canada in the year of accrual. On July 1, 2015, while Mr. X is still a resident of Canada, Mr. X receives a lump-sum distribution of 1,270 from his Roth IRA. The 1,120 that was in the Roth IRA on June 30, 2010 is treated as a distribution from a pension plan that, pursuant to paragraph 1 of Article XVIII, is exempt from tax in Canada provided it would be exempt from tax in the United States under the Internal Revenue Code if paid to a resident of the United States. The remaining 150 comprises the after-tax contribution of 100 in 2010 and accretions of 50 that were subject to Canadian tax in the year of accrual.

The rules of new subparagraph 3(b) of Article XVIII also will apply to any plan or arrangement created pursuant to legislation enacted by either Contracting State after September 21, 2007 (the date of signature of the Protocol) that the competent authorities agree is similar to a Roth IRA.

Source of payments under life insurance and annuity contracts

Paragraph 1 of Article 13 also replaces paragraph 4 of Article XVIII. Subparagraph 4(a) contains the existing definition of annuity, while subparagraph 4(b) adds a source rule to address the treatment of certain payments by branches of insurance companies.

Subparagraph 4(a) provides that, for purposes of the Convention, the term "annuity" means a stated sum paid periodically at stated times during life or during a specified number of years, under an obligation to make the payments in return for adequate and full consideration other than services rendered. The term does not include a payment that is not periodic or any annuity the cost of which was deductible for tax purposes in the Contracting State where the annuity was acquired. Items excluded from the definition of "annuity" and not dealt with under another Article of the Convention are subject to the rules of Article XXII (Other Income).

Under the existing Convention, payments under life insurance and annuity contracts to a resident of Canada by a Canadian branch of a U.S. insurance company are subject to either a 15-percent withholding tax under subparagraph 2(b) of Article XVIII or, unless dealt with under another Article of the Convention, an unreduced 30-percent withholding tax under paragraph 1 of Article XXII, depending on whether the payments constitute annuities within the meaning of paragraph 4 of Article XVIII.

On July 12, 2004, the Internal Revenue Service issued Revenue Ruling 2004-75, 2004-2 C.B. 109, which provides in relevant part that annuity payments under, and withdrawals of cash value from, life insurance or annuity contracts issued by a foreign branch of a U.S. life insurance company are U.S.-source income that, when paid to a nonresident alien individual, is generally subject to a 30-percent withholding tax under Code sections 871(a) and 1441. Revenue Ruling 2004-97, 2004-2 C.B. 516, provided that Revenue Ruling 2004-75 would not be applied to payments that were made before January 1, 2005, provided that such payments were made pursuant to binding life insurance or annuity contracts issued on or before July 12, 2004.

Under new subparagraph 4(b) of Article XVIII, an annuity or other amount paid in respect of a life insurance or annuity contract (including a withdrawal in respect of the cash value thereof), will generally be deemed to arise in the Contracting State where the person paying the annuity or other amount (the "payer") is resident. However, if the payer, whether a resident of a Contracting State or not, has a permanent establishment in a Contracting State other than a Contracting State in which the payer is a resident, the payment will be deemed to arise in the Contracting State in which the permanent establishment is situated if both of the following requirements are satisfied: (i) the obligation giving rise to the annuity or other amount must have been incurred in connection with the permanent establishment, and (ii) the annuity or other amount must be borne by the permanent establishment. When these requirements are satisfied, payments by a Canadian branch of a U.S. insurance company will be deemed to arise in Canada.

Paragraph 2

Paragraph 2 of Article 13 of the Protocol replaces paragraph 7 of Article XVIII of the existing Convention. Paragraph 7 continues to provide a rule with respect to the taxation of a natural person on income accrued in a pension or employee benefit plan in the other Contracting State. Thus, paragraph 7 applies where an individual is a citizen or resident of a Contracting State and is a beneficiary of a trust, company, organization, or other arrangement that is a resident of the other Contracting State, where such trust, company, organization, or other arrangement is generally exempt from income taxation in that other State, and is operated exclusively to provide pension, or employee benefits. In such cases, the beneficiary may elect to defer taxation in his State of residence on income accrued in the plan until it is distributed from the plan (or from another plan in that other Contracting State to which the income is transferred pursuant to the domestic law of that other Contracting State).

Paragraph 2 of Article 13 of the Protocol makes two changes to paragraph 7 of Article XVIII of the existing Convention. The first change is that the phrase "pension, retirement or employee benefits" is changed to "pension or employee benefits" solely to reflect the fact that in certain cases, discussed above, Roth IRAs will not be treated as pensions for purposes of Article XVIII. The second change is that "under" is changed to "subject to" to make it clear that an election to defer taxation with respect to undistributed income accrued in a plan may be made whether or not the competent authority of the first-mentioned State has prescribed rules for making an election. For the U.S. rules, see Revenue Procedure 2002-23, 2002-1 C.B. 744. As of the date the Protocol was signed, the competent authority of Canada had not prescribed rules.

Paragraph 3

Paragraph 3 of Article 13 of the Protocol adds paragraphs 8 through 17 to Article XVIII to deal with cross-border pension contributions. These paragraphs are intended to remove barriers to the flow of personal services between the Contracting States that could otherwise result from discontinuities in the laws of the Contracting States regarding the deductibility of pension contributions. Such discontinuities may arise where a country allows deductions or exclusions to its residents for contributions, made by them or on their behalf, to resident pension plans, but does not allow deductions or exclusions for payments made to plans resident in another country, even if the structure and legal requirements of such plans in the two countries are similar.

There is no comparable set of rules in the OECD Model, although the issue is discussed in detail in the Commentary to Article 18 (Pensions). The 2006 U.S. Model deals with this issue in paragraphs 2 through 4 of Article 18 (Pension Funds).

Workers on short-term assignments in the other Contracting State

Paragraphs 8 and 9 of Article XVIII address the case of a short-term assignment where an individual who is participating in a "qualifying retirement plan" (as defined in paragraph 15 of Article XVIII) in one Contracting State (the "home State") performs services as an employee for a limited period of time in the other Contracting State (the "host State"). If certain requirements are satisfied, contributions made to, or benefits accrued under, the plan by or on behalf of the individual will be deductible or excludible in computing the individual's income in the host State. In addition, contributions made to the plan by the individual's employer will be allowed as a deduction in computing the employer's profits in the host State.

In order for paragraph 8 to apply, the remuneration that the individual receives with respect to the services performed in the host State must be taxable in the host State. This means, for example, that where the United States is the host State, paragraph 8 would not apply if the remuneration that the individual receives with respect to the services performed in the United States is exempt from taxation in the United States under Code section 893.

The individual also must have been participating in the plan, or in another similar plan for which the plan was substituted, immediately before he began performing services in the host State. The rule regarding a successor plan would apply if, for example, the employer has been acquired by another corporation that replaces the existing plan with its own plan, transferring membership in the old plan over into the new plan.

In addition, the individual must not have been a resident (as determined under Article IV (Residence)) of the host State immediately before he began performing services in the host State. It is irrelevant for purposes of paragraph 8 whether the individual becomes a resident of the host State while he performs services there. A citizen of the United States who has been a resident of Canada may be entitled to benefits under paragraph 8 if (a) he performs services in the United States for a limited period of time and (b) he was a resident of Canada immediately before he began performing such services.

Benefits are available under paragraph 8 only for so long as the individual has not performed services in the host State for the same employer (or a related employer) for more than 60 of the 120 months preceding the individual's current taxable year. The purpose of this rule is to limit the period of time for which the host State will be required to provide benefits for contributions to a plan from which it is unlikely to be able to tax the distributions. If the individual continues to perform services in the host State beyond this time limit, he is expected to become a participant in a plan in the host State. Canada's domestic law provides preferential tax treatment for employer contributions to foreign pension plans in respect of services rendered in Canada by short-term residents, but such treatment ceases once the individual has been resident in Canada for at least 60 of the preceding 72 months.

The contributions and benefits must be attributable to services performed by the individual in the host State, and must be made or accrued during the period in which the individual performs those services. This rule prevents individuals who render services in the host State for a very short period of time from making disproportionately large contributions to home State plans in order to offset the tax liability associated with the income earned in the host State. In the case where the United States is the host State, contributions will be deemed to have been made on the last day of the preceding taxable year if the payment is on account of such taxable year and is treated under U.S. law as a contribution made on the last day of the preceding taxable year.

If an individual receives benefits in the host State with respect to contributions to a plan in the home State, the services to which the contributions relate may not be taken into account for purposes of determining the individual's entitlement to benefits under any trust, company, organization, or other arrangement that is a resident of the host State, generally exempt from income taxation in that State and operated to provide pension or retirement benefits. The purpose of this rule is to prevent double benefits for contributions to both a home State plan and a host State plan with respect to the same services. Thus, for example, an individual who is working temporarily in the United States and making contributions to a qualifying retirement plan in Canada with respect to services performed in the United States may not make contributions to an individual retirement account (within the meaning of Code section 408(a)) in the United States with respect to the same services.

Paragraph 8 states that it applies only to the extent that the contributions or benefits would qualify for tax relief in the home State if the individual were a resident of and performed services in that State. Thus, benefits would be limited in the same fashion

33

as if the individual continued to be a resident of the home State. However, paragraph 9 provides that if the host State is the United States and the individual is a citizen of the United States, the benefits granted to the individual under paragraph 8 may not exceed the benefits that would be allowed by the United States to its residents for contributions to, or benefits otherwise accrued under, a generally corresponding pension or retirement plan established in and recognized for tax purposes by the United States. Thus, the lower of the two limits applies. This rule ensures that U.S. citizens working temporarily in the United States and participating in a Canadian plan will not get more favorable U.S. tax treatment than U.S. citizens participating in a U.S. plan.

Where the United States is the home State, the amount of contributions that may be excluded from the employee's income under paragraph 8 for Canadian purposes is limited to the U.S. dollar amount specified in Code section 415 or the U.S. dollar amount specified in Code section $402(g)(1)$ to the extent contributions are made from the employee's compensation. For this purpose, the dollar limit specified in Code section $402(g)(1)$ means the amount applicable under Code section $402(g)(1)$ (including the age 50 catch-up amount in Code section $402(g)(1)(C)$) or, if applicable, the parallel dollar limit applicable under Code section $457(e)(15)$ plus the age 50 catch-up amount under Code section $414(v)(2)(B)(i)$ for a Code section $457(g)$ trust.

Where Canada is the home State, the amount of contributions that may be excluded from the employee's income under paragraph 8 for U.S. purposes is subject to the limitations specified in subsections $146(5)$, $147(8)$, $147.1(8)$ and (9) and $147.2(1)$ and (4) of the Income Tax Act and paragraph $8503(4)(a)$ of the Income Tax Regulations, as applicable. If the employee is a citizen of the United States, then the amount of contributions that may be excluded is the lesser of the amounts determined under the limitations specified in the previous sentence and the amounts specified in the previous paragraph.

The provisions described above provide benefits to employees. Paragraph 8 also provides that contributions made to the home State plan by an individual's employer will be allowed as a deduction in computing the employer's profits in the host State, even though such a deduction might not be allowable under the domestic law of the host State. This rule applies whether the employer is a resident of the host State or a permanent establishment that the employer has in the host State. The rule also applies to contributions by a person related to the individual's employer, such as contributions by a parent corporation for its subsidiary, that are treated under the law of the host State as contributions by the individual's employer. For example, if an individual who is participating in a qualifying retirement plan in Canada performs services for a limited period of time in the United States for a U.S. subsidiary of a Canadian company, a contribution to the Canadian plan by the parent company in Canada that is treated under U.S. law as a contribution by the U.S. subsidiary would be covered by the rule.

The amount of the allowable deduction is to be determined under the laws of the home State. Thus, where the United States is the home State, the amount of the deduction that is allowable in Canada will be subject to the limitations of Code section 404 (including the Code section $401(a)(17)$ and 415 limitations). Where Canada is the home State, the amount of the deduction that is allowable in the United States is subject to the limitations specified in subsections $147(8)$, $147.1(8)$ and (9) and $147.2(1)$ of the Income Tax Act, as applicable.

Cross-border commuters

Paragraphs 10, 11, and 12 of Article XVIII address the case of a commuter who is a resident of one Contracting State (the "residence State") and performs services as an employee in the other Contracting State (the "services State") and is a member of a "qualifying retirement plan" (as defined in paragraph 15 of Article XVIII) in the services State. If certain requirements are satisfied, contributions made to, or benefits accrued under, the qualifying retirement plan by or on behalf of the individual will be deductible or excludible in computing the individual's income in the residence State.

In order for paragraph 10 to apply, the individual must perform services as an employee in the services State the remuneration from which is taxable in the services State and is borne by either an employer who is a resident of the services State or by a permanent establishment that the employer has in the services State. The contributions and benefits must be attributable to those services and must be made or accrued during the period in which the individual performs those services. In the case where the United States is the residence State, contributions will be deemed to have been made on the last day of the preceding taxable year if the payment is on account of such taxable year and is treated under U.S. law as a contribution made on the last day of the preceding taxable year.

Paragraph 10 states that it applies only to the extent that the contributions or benefits qualify for tax relief in the services State. Thus, the benefits granted in the residence State are available only to the extent that the contributions or benefits accrued qualify for relief in the services State. Where the United States is the services State, the amount of contributions that may be excluded under paragraph 10 is the U.S. dollar amount specified in Code section 415 or the U.S. dollar amount specified in Code section 402(g)(1) (as defined above) to the extent contributions are made from the employee's compensation. Where Canada is the services State, the amount of contributions that may be excluded from the employee's income under paragraph 10 is subject to the limitations specified in subsections 146(5), 147(8), 147.1(8) and (9) and 147.2(1) and (4) of the Income Tax Act and paragraph 8503(4)(a) of the Income Tax Regulations, as applicable.

However, paragraphs 11 and 12 further provide that the benefits granted under paragraph 10 by the residence State may not exceed certain benefits that would be allowable under the domestic law of the residence State.

Paragraph 11 provides that where Canada is the residence State, the amount of contributions otherwise allowable as a deduction under paragraph 10 may not exceed the individual's deduction limit for contributions to registered retirement savings plans (RRSPs) remaining after taking into account the amount of contributions to RRSPs deducted by the individual under the law of Canada for the year. The amount deducted by the individual under paragraph 10 will be taken into account in computing the individual's deduction limit for subsequent taxation years for contributions to RRSPs. This rule prevents double benefits for contributions to both an RRSP and a qualifying retirement plan in the United States with respect to the same services.

Paragraph 12 provides that if the United States is the residence State, the benefits granted to an individual under paragraph 10 may not exceed the benefits that would be allowed by the United States to its residents for contributions to, or benefits otherwise accrued under, a generally corresponding pension or retirement plan established in and recognized for tax purposes by the United States. For purposes of determining an individual's eligibility to participate in and receive tax benefits with respect to a pension or retirement plan or other retirement arrangement in the United States, contributions made to, or benefits accrued under, a qualifying retirement plan in Canada by or on behalf of the individual are treated as contributions or benefits under a generally corresponding pension or retirement plan established in and recognized for tax purposes by the United States. Thus, for example, the qualifying retirement plan in Canada would be taken into account for purposes of determining whether the individual is an "active participant" within the meaning of Code section 219(g)(5), with the result that the individual's ability to make deductible contributions to an individual retirement account in the United States would be limited.

Paragraph 10 does not address employer deductions because the employer is located in the services State and is already eligible for deductions under the domestic law of the services State.

U.S. citizens resident in Canada

Paragraphs 13 and 14 of Article XVIII address the special case of a U.S. citizen who is a resident of Canada (as determined under Article IV (Residence)) and who performs services as an employee in Canada and participates in a qualifying retirement plan (as defined in paragraph 15 of Article XVIII) in Canada. If certain requirements are satisfied, contributions made to, or benefits accrued under, a qualifying retirement plan in Canada by or on behalf of the U.S. citizen will be deductible or excludible in computing his or her taxable income in the United States. These provisions are generally consistent with paragraph 4 of Article 18 of the U.S. Model treaty.

In order for paragraph 13 to apply, the U.S. citizen must perform services as an employee in Canada the remuneration from which is taxable in Canada and is borne by an employer who is a resident of Canada or by a permanent establishment that the employer has in Canada. The contributions and benefits must be attributable to those services and must be made or accrued during the period in which the U.S. citizen performs those services. Contributions will be deemed to have been made on the last day of the preceding taxable year if the payment is on account of such taxable year and is treated under U.S. law as a contribution made on the last day of the preceding taxable year.

Paragraph 13 states that it applies only to the extent the contributions or benefits qualify for tax relief in Canada. However, paragraph 14 provides that the benefits granted under paragraph 13 may not exceed the benefits that would be allowed by the United States to its residents for contributions to, or benefits otherwise accrued under, a generally corresponding pension or retirement plan established in and recognized for tax purposes by the United States. Thus, the lower of the two limits applies. This rule ensures that a U.S. citizen living and working in Canada does not receive better U.S. treatment than a U.S. citizen living and working in the United States. The amount of contributions that may be excluded from the employee's income under paragraph 13 is the U.S. dollar amount specified in Code section 415 or the U.S. dollar amount specified in Code section 402(g)(1) (as defined above) to the extent contributions are made from the employee's compensation. In addition, pursuant to Code section 911(d)(6), an individual may not claim benefits under paragraph 13 with respect to services the remuneration for which is excluded from the individual's gross income under Code section 911(a).

For purposes of determining the individual's eligibility to participate in and receive tax benefits with respect to a pension or retirement plan or other retirement arrangement established in and recognized for tax purposes by the United States, contributions made to, or benefits accrued under, a qualifying retirement plan in Canada by or on behalf of the individual are treated as contributions or benefits under a generally corresponding pension or retirement plan established in and recognized for tax purposes by the United States. Thus, for example, the qualifying retirement plan in Canada would be taken into account for purposes of determining whether the individual is an "active participant" within the meaning of Code section 219(g)(5), with the result that the individual's ability to make deductible contributions to an individual retirement account in the United States would be limited.

Paragraph 13 does not address employer deductions because the employer is located in Canada and is already eligible for deductions under the domestic law of Canada.

Definition of "qualifying retirement plan"

Paragraph 15 of Article XVIII provides that for purposes of paragraphs 8 through 14, a "qualifying retirement plan" in a Contracting State is a trust, company, organization, or other arrangement that (a) is a resident of that State, generally exempt from income taxation in that State and operated primarily to provide pension or retirement benefits; (b) is not an individual arrangement in respect of which the individual's employer has no involvement; and (c) the competent authority of the other Contracting State agrees generally corresponds to a pension or retirement plan established in and recognized for tax purposes in that State. Thus, U.S. individual retirement accounts (IRAs) and Canadian registered retirement savings plans (RRSPs) are not treated as qualifying retirement plans unless addressed in paragraph 10 of the General Note (as discussed below). In addition, a Canadian retirement compensation arrangement (RCA) is not a qualifying retirement plan because it is not considered to be generally exempt from income taxation in Canada.

Paragraph 10 of the General Note provides that the types of Canadian plans that constitute qualifying retirement plans for purposes of paragraph 15 include the following and any identical or substantially similar plan that is established pursuant to legislation introduced after the date of signature of the Protocol (September 21, 2007): registered pension plans under section 147.1 of the Income Tax Act, registered retirement savings plans under section 146 that are part of a group arrangement described in subsection 204.2(1.32), deferred profit sharing plans under section 147, and any registered retirement savings plan under section 146, or registered retirement income fund under section 146.3, that is funded exclusively by rollover contributions from one or more of the preceding plans.

Paragraph 10 of the General Note also provides that the types of U.S. plans that constitute qualifying retirement plans for purposes of paragraph 15 include the following and any identical or substantially similar plan that is established pursuant to legislation introduced after the date of signature of the Protocol (September 21, 2007): qualified plans under Code section 401(a) (including Code section 401(k) arrangements), individual retirement plans that are part of a simplified employee pension plan that satisfies Code section 408(k), Code section 408(p) simple retirement accounts, Code section 403(a) qualified annuity plans, Code section 403(b) plans, Code section 457(g) trusts providing benefits under Code section 457(b) plans, the Thrift Savings Fund (Code section 7701(j)), and any individual retirement account under Code section 408(a) that is funded exclusively by rollover contributions from one or more of the preceding plans.

If a particular plan in one Contracting State is of a type specified in paragraph 10 of the General Note with respect to paragraph 15 of Article XVIII, it will not be necessary for taxpayers to obtain a determination from the competent authority of the other Contracting State that the plan generally corresponds to a pension or retirement plan established in and recognized for tax purposes in that State. A taxpayer who believes a particular plan in one Contracting State that is not described in paragraph 10 of the General Note nevertheless satisfies the requirements of paragraph 15 may request a determination from the competent authority of the other Contracting State that the plan generally corresponds to a pension or retirement plan established in and recognized for tax purposes in that State. In the case of the United States, such a determination must be requested under Revenue Procedure 2006-54, 2006-49 I.R.B. 655 (or any applicable analogous provision). In the case of Canada, the current version of Information Circular 71-17 provides guidance on obtaining assistance from the Canadian competent authority.

Source rule

Paragraph 16 of Article XVIII provides that a distribution from a pension or retirement plan that is reasonably attributable to a contribution or benefit for which a benefit was allowed pursuant to paragraph 8, 10, or 13 of Article XVIII will be deemed to arise in the Contracting State in which the plan is established. This ensures that the Contracting State in which the plan is established will have the right to tax the gross amount of the distribution under subparagraph 2(a) of Article XVIII, even if a portion of the services to which the distribution relates were not performed in such Contracting State.

Partnerships

Paragraph 17 of Article XVIII provides that paragraphs 8 through 16 of Article XVIII apply, with such modifications as the circumstances require, as though the relationship between a partnership that carries on a business, and an individual who is a member of the partnership, were that of employer and employee. This rule is needed because paragraphs 8, 10, and 13, by their terms, apply only with respect to contributions made to, or benefits accrued under, qualifying retirement plans by or on behalf of individuals who perform services as an employee. Thus, benefits are not available with respect to retirement plans for self-employed individuals, who may be deemed under U.S. law to be employees for certain pension purposes. Paragraph 17 ensures that partners participating in a plan established by their partnership may be eligible for the benefits provided by paragraphs 8, 10, and 13.

Relationship to other Articles

Paragraphs 8, 10, and 13 of Article XVIII are not subject to the saving clause of paragraph 2 of Article XXIX (Miscellaneous Rules) by reason of the exception in subparagraph 3(a) of Article XXIX.

Article 14

Consistent with Articles 9 and 10 of the Protocol, Article 14 of the Protocol amends Article XIX (Government Service) of the Convention by deleting the reference to "Article XIV (Independent Personal Services)" and replacing such reference with the reference to "Article VII (Business Profits)" and by reflecting the new name of Article XV (Income from Employment).

Article 15

Article 15 of the Protocol replaces Article XX (Students) of the Convention. Article XX provides rules for host-country taxation of visiting students and business trainees. Persons who meet the tests of Article XX will be exempt from tax in the State that they are visiting with respect to designated classes of income. Several conditions must be satisfied in order for an individual to be entitled to the benefits of this Article.

First, the visitor must have been, either at the time of his arrival in the host State or immediately before, a resident of the other Contracting State.

Second, the purpose of the visit must be the full-time education or training of the visitor. Thus, if the visitor comes principally to work in the host State but also is a part-time student, he would not be entitled to the benefits of this Article, even with respect to any payments he may receive from abroad for his maintenance or education, and regardless of whether or not he is in a degree program. Whether a student is to be considered full-time will be determined by the rules of the educational institution at which he is studying.

The host State exemption in Article XX applies to payments received by the student or business trainee for the purpose of his maintenance, education or training that arise outside the host State. A payment will be considered to arise outside the host State if the payer is located outside the host State. Thus, if an employer from one of the Contracting States sends an employee to the other Contracting State for full-time training, the payments the trainee receives from abroad from his employer for his maintenance or training while he is present in the host State will be exempt from tax in the host State. Where appropriate, substance prevails over form in determining the identity of the payer. Thus, for example, payments made directly or indirectly by a U.S. person with whom the visitor is training, but which have been routed through a source outside the United States (*e.g.*, a foreign subsidiary), are not treated as arising outside the United States for this purpose.

In the case of an apprentice or business trainee, the benefits of Article XX will extend only for a period of one year from the time that the individual first arrives in the host country for the purpose of the individual's training. If, however, an apprentice or trainee remains in the host country for a second year, thus losing the benefits of the Article, he would not retroactively lose the benefits of the Article for the first year.

Relationship to other Articles

The saving clause of paragraph 2 of Article XXIX (Miscellaneous Rules) does not apply to Article XX with respect to an individual who neither is a citizen of the host State nor has been admitted for permanent residence there. The saving clause, however, does apply with respect to citizens and permanent residents of the host State. Thus, a U.S. citizen who is a resident of Canada and who visits the United States as a full-time student at an accredited university will not be exempt from U.S. tax on remittances from abroad that otherwise constitute U.S. taxable income. However, an individual who is not a U.S. citizen, and who visits the United States as a student and remains long enough to become a resident under U.S. law, but does not become a permanent resident (*i.e.*, does not acquire a green card), will be entitled to the full benefits of the Article.

Article 16

Article 16 of the Protocol revises Article XXI (Exempt Organizations) of the existing Convention.

Paragraph 1

Paragraph 1 amends Article XXI by renumbering paragraphs 4, 5, and 6 as 5, 6, and 7, respectively.

Paragraph 2

Paragraph 2 replaces paragraphs 1 through 3 of Article XXI with four new paragraphs. In general, the provisions of former paragraphs 1 through 3 have been retained.

New paragraph 1 provides that a religious, scientific, literary, educational, or charitable organization resident in a Contracting State shall be exempt from tax on income arising in the other Contracting State but only to the extent that such income is exempt from taxation in the Contracting State in which the organization is resident.

New paragraph 2 retains the provisions of former subparagraph 2(a), and provides that a trust, company, organization, or other arrangement that is resident in a Contracting State and operated exclusively to administer or provide pension, retirement or employee benefits or benefits for the self-employed under one or more funds or plans established to provide pension or retirement benefits or other employee benefits is exempt from taxation on dividend and interest income arising in the other Contracting State in a taxable year, if the income of such organization or other arrangement is generally exempt from taxation for that year in the Contracting State in which it is resident.

New paragraph 3 replaces and expands the scope of former subparagraph 2(b) Former subparagraph 2(b) provided that, subject to the provisions of paragraph 3 (new paragraph 4), a trust, company, organization or other arrangement that was a resident of a Contracting State, generally exempt from income taxation in that State and operated exclusively to earn income for the benefit of one or more organizations described in subparagraph 2(a) (new paragraph 2) was exempt from taxation on dividend and interest income arising in the other Contracting State in a taxable year. The Internal Revenue Service concluded in private letter rulings (PLR 200111027 and PLR 200111037) that a pooled investment fund that included as investors one or more organizations described in paragraph 1 could not qualify for benefits under former subparagraph 2(b). New paragraph 3 now allows organizations described in paragraph 1 to invest in pooled funds with trusts, companies, organizations, or other arrangements described in new paragraph 2.

Former subparagraph 2(b) did not exempt income earned by a trust, company or other arrangement for the benefit of religious, scientific, literary, educational or charitable organizations exempt from tax under paragraph 1. Therefore, the Protocol expands the scope of paragraph 3 to include such income.

As noted above with respect to Article X (Dividends), paragraph 3 of the General Note explains that distributions from Canadian income trusts and royalty trusts that are treated as dividends as a result of changes to Canada's law regarding taxation of income and royalty trusts shall be treated as dividends for the purposes of Article X. Accordingly, such distributions will also be entitled to the benefits of Article XXI.

New paragraph 4 replaces paragraph 3 and provides that the exemptions provided by paragraphs 1, 2, 3 do not apply with respect to the income of a trust, company, organization or other arrangement from carrying on a trade or business or from a related person, other than a person referred to in paragraph 1, 2 or 3. The term "related person" is not necessarily defined by paragraph 2 of Article IX (Related Person).

Article 17

Article 17 of the Protocol amends Article XXII (Other Income) of the Convention by adding a new paragraph 4. Article XXII generally assigns taxing jurisdiction over income not dealt with in the other articles (Articles VI through XXI) of the Convention.

New paragraph 4 provides a specific rule for residence State taxation of compensation derived in respect of a guarantee of indebtedness. New paragraph 4 provides that compensation derived by a resident of a Contracting State in respect of the provision of a guarantee of indebtedness shall be taxable only in that State, unless the compensation is business profits attributable to a permanent establishment situated in the other Contracting State, in which case the provisions of Article VII (Business Profits) shall apply. The clarification that Article VII shall apply when the compensation is considered business profits was included at the request of the United States. Compensation paid to a financial services entity to provide a guarantee in the ordinary course of its business of providing such guarantees to customers constitutes business profits dealt with under the provisions of Article VII. However, provision of guarantees with respect to debt of related parties is ordinarily not an independent economic undertaking that would generate business profits, and thus compensation in respect of such related-party guarantees is, in most cases, covered by Article XXII.

Article 18

Article 18 of the Protocol amends paragraph 2 of Article XXIII (Capital) of the Convention by deleting language contained in that paragraph consistent with the changes made by Article 9 of the Protocol.

Article 19

Article 19 of the Protocol deletes subparagraph 2(b) of Article XXIV (Elimination of Double Taxation) of the Convention and replaces it with a new subparagraph.

New subparagraph 2(b) allows a Canadian company receiving a dividend from a U.S. resident company of which it owns at least 10 percent of the voting stock, a credit against Canadian income tax of the appropriate amount of income tax paid or accrued to the United States by the dividend paying company with respect to the profits out of which the dividends are paid. The third Protocol to the Convention, signed March 17, 1995, had amended subparagraph (b) to allow a Canadian company to deduct in computing its Canadian taxable income any dividend received by it out of the exempt surplus of a foreign affiliate which is a resident of the United States. This change is consistent with current Canadian tax treaty practice: it does not indicate any present intention to change Canada's "exempt surplus" rules, and those rules remain in effect.

Article 20

Article 20 of the Protocol revises Article XXV (Non-Discrimination) of the existing Convention to bring that Article into closer conformity to U.S. tax treaty policy.

Paragraphs 1 and 2

Paragraph 1 replaces paragraph 1 of Article XXV of the existing Convention. New paragraph 1 provides that a national of one Contracting State may not be subject to taxation or connected requirements in the other Contracting State that are more burdensome than the taxes and connected requirements imposed upon a national of that other State in the same circumstances. The OECD Model would prohibit taxation that is "other than or more burdensome" than that imposed on U.S. persons. Paragraph 1 omits the words "other than or" because the only relevant question under this provision should be whether the requirement imposed on a national of the other Contracting State is more burdensome. A requirement may be different from the requirements imposed on U.S. nationals without being more burdensome.

The term "national" in relation to a Contracting State is defined in subparagraph 1(k) of Article III (General Definitions). The term includes both individuals and juridical persons. A national of a Contracting State is afforded protection under this paragraph even if the national is not a resident of either Contracting State. Thus, a U.S. citizen who is resident in a third country is entitled, under this paragraph, to the same treatment in Canada as a national of Canada in the same or similar circumstances (*i.e.*, one who is resident in a third State).

Whether or not the two persons are both taxable on worldwide income is a significant circumstance for this purpose. For this reason, paragraph 1 specifically refers to taxation or any requirement connected therewith, particularly with respect to taxation on worldwide income, as relevant circumstances. This language means that the United States is not obliged to apply the same taxing regime to a national of Canada who is not resident in the United States as it applies to a U.S. national who is not resident in the United States. U.S. citizens who are not resident in the United States but who are, nevertheless, subject to U.S. tax on their worldwide income are not in the same circumstances with respect to U.S. taxation as citizens of Canada who are not U.S. residents. Thus, for example, Article XXV would not entitle a national of Canada residing in a third country to taxation at graduated rates on U.S.-source dividends or other investment income that applies to a U.S. citizen residing in the same third country.

Because of the increased coverage of paragraph 1 with respect to the treatment of nationals wherever they are resident, paragraph 2 of this Article no longer has application, and therefore has been omitted.

Paragraph 3

Paragraph 3 makes changes to renumbered paragraph 3 of Article XXV in order to conform with Article 10 of the Protocol by deleting the reference to "Article XV (Dependent Personal Services)" and replacing it with a reference to "Article XV (Income from Employment)."

Article 21

Paragraph 1 of Article 21 of the Protocol replaces paragraph 6 of Article XXVI (Mutual Agreement Procedure) of the Convention with new paragraphs 6 and 7. New paragraphs 6 and 7 provide a mandatory binding arbitration proceeding (Arbitration Proceeding). The Arbitration Note details additional rules and procedures that apply to a case considered under the arbitration provisions.

New paragraph 6 provides that a case shall be resolved through arbitration when the competent authorities have endeavored but are unable through negotiation to reach a complete agreement regarding a case and the following three conditions are satisfied. First, tax returns have been filed with at least one of the Contracting States with respect to the taxable years at issue in the case. Second, the case (i) involves the application of one or more Articles that the competent authorities have agreed in an exchange of notes shall be the subject of arbitration and is not a case that the competent authorities agree before the date on which an Arbitration Proceeding would otherwise have begun, is not suitable for determination by arbitration; or (ii) is a case that the competent authorities agree is suitable for determination by arbitration. Third, all concerned persons and their authorized representatives agree, according to the provisions of subparagraph 7(d), not to disclose to any other person any information received during the course of the Arbitration Proceeding from either Contracting State or the arbitration board, other than the determination of the board (confidentiality agreement). The confidentiality agreement may also be executed by any concerned person that has the legal authority to bind any other concerned person on the matter. For example, a parent corporation with the legal authority to bind its subsidiary with respect to confidentiality may execute a comprehensive confidentiality agreement on its own behalf and that of its subsidiary.

The United States and Canada have agreed in the Arbitration Note to submit cases regarding the application of one or more of the following Articles to mandatory binding arbitration under the provisions of paragraphs 6 and 7 of Article XXVI: IV (Residence), but only insofar as it relates to the residence of a natural person, V (Permanent Establishment), VII (Business Profits), IX (Related Persons), and XII (Royalties) (but only (i) insofar as Article XII might apply in transactions involving related persons to whom Article IX might apply, or (ii) to an allocation of amounts between royalties that are taxable under paragraph 2 thereof and royalties that are exempt under paragraph 3 thereof). The competent authorities may, however, agree, before the date on which an Arbitration Proceeding would otherwise have begun, that a particular case is not suitable for arbitration.

New paragraph 7 provides six subparagraphs that detail the general rules and definitions to be used in applying the arbitration provisions.

Subparagraph 7(a) provides that the term "concerned person" means the person that brought the case to competent authority for consideration under Article XXVI (Mutual Agreement Procedure) and includes all other persons, if any, whose tax liability to either Contracting State may be directly affected by a mutual agreement arising from that consideration. For example, a concerned person does not only include a U.S. corporation that brings a transfer pricing case with respect to a transaction entered into with its Canadian subsidiary for resolution to the U.S. competent authority, but also the Canadian subsidiary, which may have a correlative adjustment as a result of the resolution of the case.

Subparagraph 7(c) provides that an Arbitration Proceeding begins on the later of two dates: two years from the "commencement date" of the case (unless the competent authorities have previously agreed to a different date), or the earliest date upon which all concerned persons have entered into a confidentiality agreement and the agreements have been received by both competent authorities. The "commencement date" of the case is defined by subparagraph 7(b) as the earliest date the information necessary to undertake substantive consideration for a mutual agreement has been received by both competent authorities.

Paragraph 16 of the Arbitration Note provides that each competent authority will confirm in writing to the other competent authority and to the concerned persons the date of its receipt of the information necessary to undertake substantive consideration for a mutual agreement. In the case of the United States, this information is (i) the information that must be submitted to the U.S. competent authority under Section 4.05 of Rev. Proc. 2006-54, 2006-49 I.R.B. 1035 (or any applicable successor publication), and (ii) for cases initially submitted as a request for an Advance Pricing Agreement, the information that must be submitted to the Internal Revenue Service under Rev. Proc. 2006-9, 2006-2 I.R.B. 278 (or any applicable successor publication). In the case of Canada, this information is the information required to be submitted to the Canadian competent authority under Information Circular 71-17 (or any applicable successor publication). The information shall not be considered received until both competent authorities have received copies of all materials submitted to either Contracting State by the concerned person(s) in connection with the mutual agreement procedure. It is understood that confirmation of the "information necessary to undertake substantive consideration for a mutual agreement" is envisioned to ordinarily occur within 30 days after the necessary information is provided to the competent authority.

The Arbitration Note also provides for several procedural rules once an Arbitration Proceeding under paragraph 6 of Article XXVI ("Proceeding") has commenced, but the competent authorities may modify or supplement these rules as necessary. In addition, the arbitration board may adopt any procedures necessary for the conduct of its business, provided the procedures are not inconsistent with any provision of Article XXVI of the Convention.

Paragraph 5 of the Arbitration Note provides that each Contracting State has 60 days from the date on which the Arbitration Proceeding begins to send a written communication to the other Contracting State appointing one member of the arbitration board. Within 60 days of the date the second of such communications is sent, these two board members will appoint a third member to serve as the chair of the board. It is agreed that this third member ordinarily should not be a citizen of either of the Contracting States.

In the event that any members of the board are not appointed (including as a result of the failure of the two members appointed by the Contracting States to agree on a third member) by the requisite date, the remaining members are appointed by the highest ranking member of the Secretariat at the Centre for Tax Policy and Administration of the Organisation for Economic Co-operation and Development (OECD) who is not a citizen of either Contracting State, by written notice to both Contracting States within 60 days of the date of such failure.

Paragraph 7 of the Arbitration Note establishes deadlines for submission of materials by the Contracting States to the arbitration board. Each competent authority has 60 days from the date of appointment of the chair to submit a Proposed Resolution describing the proposed disposition of the specific monetary amounts of income, expense or taxation at issue in the case, and a supporting Position Paper. Copies of each State's submissions are to be provided by the board to the other Contracting State on the date the later of the submissions is submitted to the board. Each of the Contracting States may submit a Reply Submission to the board within 120 days of the appointment of the chair to address points raised in the other State's Proposed Resolution or Position Paper. If one Contracting State fails to submit a Proposed Resolution within the requisite time, the Proposed Resolution of the other Contracting State is deemed to be the determination of the arbitration board. Additional information may be supplied to the arbitration board by a Contracting State only at the request of the arbitration board. The board will provide copies of any such requested information, along with the board's request, to the other Contracting State on the date the request is made or the response is received.

All communication with the board is to be in writing between the chair of the board and the designated competent authorities with the exception of communication regarding logistical matters.

In making its determination, the arbitration board will apply the following authorities as necessary: (i) the provisions of the Convention, (ii) any agreed commentaries or explanation of the Contracting States concerning the Convention as amended, (iii) the laws of the Contracting States to the extent they are not inconsistent with each other, and (iv) any OECD Commentary, Guidelines or Reports regarding relevant analogous portions of the OECD Model Tax Convention.

The arbitration board must deliver a determination in writing to the Contracting States within six months of the appointment of the chair. The determination must be one of the two Proposed Resolutions submitted by the Contracting States. The determination shall provide a determination regarding only the amount of income, expense or tax reportable to the Contracting States. The determination has no precedential value and consequently the rationale behind a board's determination would not be beneficial and shall not be provided by the board.

Paragraph 11 of the Arbitration Note provides that, unless any concerned person does not accept the decision of the arbitration board, the determination of the board constitutes a resolution by mutual agreement under Article XXVI and, consequently, is binding on both Contracting States. Each concerned person must, within 30 days of receiving the determination from the competent authority to which the case was first presented, advise that competent authority whether the person accepts the determination. The failure to advise the competent authority within the requisite time is considered a rejection of the determination. If a determination is rejected, the case cannot be the subject of a subsequent MAP procedure on the same issue(s) determined by the panel, including a subsequent Arbitration Proceeding. After the commencement of an Arbitration Proceeding but before a decision of the board has been accepted by all concerned persons, the competent authorities may reach a mutual agreement to resolve the case and terminate the Proceeding.

For purposes of the Arbitration Proceeding, the members of the arbitration board and their staffs shall be considered "persons or authorities" to whom information may be disclosed under Article XXVII (Exchange of Information). The Arbitration Note provides that all materials prepared in the course of, or relating to, the Arbitration Proceeding are considered information exchanged between the Contracting States. No information relating to the Arbitration Proceeding or the board's determination may be disclosed by members of the arbitration board or their staffs or by either competent authority, except as permitted by the Convention and the domestic laws of the Contracting States. Members of the arbitration board and their staffs must agree in statements sent to each of the Contracting States in confirmation of their appointment to the arbitration board to abide by and be subject to the confidentiality and nondisclosure provisions of Article XXVII of the Convention and the applicable domestic laws of the Contracting States, with the most restrictive of the provisions applying.

The applicable domestic law of the Contracting States determines the treatment of any interest or penalties associated with a competent authority agreement achieved through arbitration.

In general, fees and expenses are borne equally by the Contracting States, including the cost of translation services. However, meeting facilities, related resources, financial management, other logistical support, and general and administrative coordination of the Arbitration Proceeding will be provided, at its own cost, by the Contracting State that initiated the Mutual Agreement Procedure. The fees and expenses of members of the board will be set in accordance with the International Centre for Settlement of Investment Disputes (ICSID) Schedule of Fees for arbitrators (in effect on the date on which the arbitration board proceedings begin). All other costs are to be borne by the Contracting State that incurs them. Since arbitration of MAP cases is intended to assist taxpayers in resolving a governmental difference of opinion regarding the taxation of their income, and is merely an extension of the competent authority process, no fees will be chargeable to a taxpayer in connection with arbitration.

Article 22

Article 22 of the Protocol amends Article XXVI A (Assistance in Collection) of the existing Convention. Article XXVI A sets forth provisions under which the United States and Canada have agreed to assist each other in the collection of taxes.

Paragraph 1

Paragraph 1 replaces subparagraph 8(a) of Article XXVI A. In general, new subparagraph 8(a) provides the circumstances under which no assistance is to be given under the Article for a claim in respect of an individual taxpayer. New subparagraph 8(a) contains language that is in substance the same as subparagraph 8(a) of Article XXVI A of the existing Convention. However, the revised subparagraph also provides that no assistance in collection is to be given for a revenue claim from a taxable period that ended before November 9, 1995 in respect of an individual taxpayer, if the taxpayer became a citizen of the requested State at any time before November 9, 1995 and is such a citizen at the time the applicant State applies for collection of the claim.

The additional language is intended to avoid the potentially discriminating application of former subparagraph 8(a) as applied to persons who were not citizens of the requested State in the taxable period to which a particular collection request related, but who became citizens of the requested State at a time prior to the entry into force of Article XXVI A as set forth in the third protocol signed March 17, 1995. New subparagraph 8(a) addresses this situation by treating the citizenship of a person in the requested State at anytime prior to November 9, 1995 as comparable to citizenship in the requested State during the period for which the claim for assistance relates if 1) the person is a citizen of the requested state at the time of the request for assistance in collection, and 2) the request relates to a taxable period ending prior to November 9, 1995. As is provided in subparagraph 3(g) of Article 27, this change will have effect for revenue claims finally determined after November 9, 1985, the effective date of the adoption of collection assistance in the third protocol signed March 17, 1995.

Paragraph 2

Paragraph 2 replaces paragraph 9 of Article XXVI A of the Convention. Under paragraph 1 of Article XXVI A, each Contracting State generally agrees to lend assistance and support to the other in the collection of revenue claims. The term "revenue claim" is defined in paragraph 1 to include all taxes referred to in paragraph 9 of the Article, as well as interest, costs, additions to such taxes, and civil penalties. New paragraph 9 provides that, notwithstanding the provisions of Article II (Taxes Covered) of the Convention, Article XXVI A shall apply to all categories of taxes collected, and to contributions to social security and employment insurance premiums levied, by or on behalf of the Government of a Contracting State. Prior to the Protocol, paragraph 9 did not contain a specific reference to contributions to social security and employment insurance premiums. Although the prior language covered U.S. federal social security and unemployment taxes, the language did not cover Canada's social security (*e.g.*, Canada Pension Plan) and employment insurance programs, contributions to which are not considered taxes under Canadian law and therefore would not otherwise have come within the scope of the paragraph.

Article 23

Article 23 of the Protocol replaces Article XXVII (Exchange of Information) of the Convention.

Paragraph 1 of Article XXVII

New paragraph 1 of Article XXVII is substantially the same as paragraph 1 of Article XXVII of the existing Convention. Paragraph 1 authorizes the competent authorities to exchange information as may be relevant for carrying out the provisions of the Convention or the domestic laws of Canada and the United States concerning taxes covered by the Convention, insofar as the taxation under those domestic laws is not contrary to the Convention. New paragraph 1 changes the phrase "is relevant" to "may be relevant" to clarify that the language incorporates the standard in Code section 7602 which authorizes the Internal Revenue Service to examine "any books, papers, records, or other data which *may be relevant* or material." (Emphasis added.) In *United States v. Arthur Young & Co.*, 465 U.S. 805, 814 (1984), the Supreme Court stated that "the language 'may be' reflects Congress's express intention to allow the Internal Revenue Service to obtain 'items of even *potential* relevance to an ongoing investigation, without reference to its admissibility.'" (Emphasis in original.) However, the language "may be" would not support a request in which a Contracting State simply asked for information regarding all bank accounts maintained by residents of that Contracting State in the other Contracting State, or even all accounts maintained by its residents with respect to a particular bank.

The authority to exchange information granted by paragraph 1 is not restricted by Article I (Personal Scope), and thus need not relate solely to persons otherwise covered by the Convention. Under paragraph 1, information may be exchanged for use in all phases of the taxation process including assessment, collection, enforcement or the determination of appeals. Thus, the competent authorities may request and provide information for cases under examination or criminal investigation, in collection, on appeals, or under prosecution.

Any information received by a Contracting State pursuant to the Convention is to be treated as secret in the same manner as information obtained under the tax laws of that State. Such information shall be disclosed only to persons or authorities, including courts and administrative bodies, involved in the assessment or collection of, the administration and enforcement in respect of, or the determination of appeals in relation to, the taxes covered by the Convention and the information may be used by such persons only for such purposes. (In accordance with paragraph 4, for the purposes of this Article the Convention applies to a broader range of taxes than those covered specifically by Article II (Taxes Covered)). Although the information received by persons described in paragraph 1 is to be treated as secret, it may be disclosed by such persons in public court proceedings or in judicial decisions.

Paragraph 1 also permits, however, a Contracting State to provide information received from the other Contracting State to its states, provinces, or local authorities, if it relates to a tax imposed by that state, province, or local authority that is substantially similar to a national-level tax covered under Article II (Taxes Covered). This provision does not authorize a Contracting State to request information on behalf of a state, province, or local authority. Paragraph 1 also authorizes the competent authorities to release information to any arbitration panel that may be established under the provisions of new paragraph 6 of Article XXVI (Mutual Agreement Procedure). Any information provided to a state, province, or local authority or to an arbitration panel is subject to the same use and disclosure provisions as is information received by the national Governments and used for their purposes.

The provisions of paragraph 1 authorize the U.S. competent authority to continue to allow legislative bodies, such as the tax-writing committees of Congress and the Government Accountability Office to examine tax return information received from Canada when such bodies or offices are engaged in overseeing the administration of U.S. tax laws or a study of the administration of U.S. tax laws pursuant to a directive of Congress. However, the secrecy requirements of paragraph 1 must be met.

It is contemplated that Article XXVII will be utilized by the competent authorities to exchange information upon request, routinely, and spontaneously.

Paragraph 2 of Article XXVII

New paragraph 2 conforms with the corresponding U.S. and OECD Model provisions. The substance of the second sentence of former paragraph 2 is found in new paragraph 6 of the Article, discussed below.

Paragraph 2 provides that if a Contracting State requests information in accordance with Article XXVII, the other Contracting State shall use its information gathering measures to obtain the requested information. The instruction to the requested State to "use its information gathering measures" to obtain the requested information communicates the same instruction to the requested State as the language of former paragraph 2 that stated that the requested State shall obtain the information "in the same way as if its own taxation was involved." Paragraph 2 makes clear that the obligation to provide information is limited by the provisions of paragraph 3, but that such limitations shall not be construed to permit a Contracting State to decline to obtain and supply information because it has no domestic tax interest in such information.

In the absence of such a paragraph, some taxpayers have argued that subparagraph 3(a) prevents a Contracting State from requesting information from a bank or fiduciary that the Contracting State does not need for its own tax purposes. This paragraph clarifies that paragraph 3 does not impose such a restriction and that a Contracting State is not limited to providing only the information that it already has in its own files.

Paragraph 3 of Article XXVII

New paragraph 3 is substantively the same as paragraph 3 of Article XXVII of the existing Convention. Paragraph 3 provides that the provisions of paragraphs 1 and 2 do not impose on Canada or the United States the obligation to carry out administrative measures at variance with the laws and administrative practice of either State; to supply information which is not obtainable under the laws or in the normal course of the administration of either State; or to supply information which would disclose any trade, business, industrial, commercial, or professional secret or trade process, or information the disclosure of which would be contrary to public policy.

Thus, a requesting State may be denied information from the other State if the information would be obtained pursuant to procedures or measures that are broader than those available in the requesting State. However, the statute of limitations of the Contracting State making the request for information should govern a request for information. Thus, the Contracting State of which the request is made should attempt to obtain the information even if its own statute of limitations has passed. In many cases, relevant information will still exist in the business records of the taxpayer or a third party, even though it is no longer required to be kept for domestic tax purposes.

While paragraph 3 states conditions under which a Contracting State is not obligated to comply with a request from the other Contracting State for information, the requested State is not precluded from providing such information, and may, at its discretion, do so subject to the limitations of its internal law.

As discussed with respect to paragraph 2, in no case shall the limitations in paragraph 3 be construed to permit a Contracting State to decline to obtain information and supply information because it has no domestic tax interest in such information.

Paragraph 4 of Article XXVII

The language of new paragraph 4 is substantially similar to former paragraph 4. New paragraph 4, however, consistent with new paragraph 1, discussed above, replaces the words "is relevant" with "may be relevant" in subparagraph 4(b).

Paragraph 4 provides that, for the purposes of Article XXVII, the Convention applies to all taxes imposed by a Contracting State, and to other taxes to which any other provision of the Convention applies, but only to the extent that the information may be relevant for the purposes of the application of that provision.

Article XXVII does not apply to taxes imposed by political subdivisions or local authorities of the Contracting States. Paragraph 4 is designed to ensure that information exchange will extend to taxes of every kind (including, for example, estate, gift, excise, and value added taxes) at the national level in the United States and Canada.

Paragraph 5 of Article XXVII

New paragraph 5 conforms with the corresponding U.S. and OECD Model provisions. Paragraph 5 provides that a Contracting State may not decline to provide information because that information is held by a financial institution, nominee or person acting in an agency or fiduciary capacity. Thus, paragraph 5 would effectively prevent a Contracting State from relying on paragraph 3 to argue that its domestic bank secrecy laws (or similar legislation relating to disclosure of financial information by financial institutions or intermediaries) override its obligation to provide information under paragraph 1. This paragraph also requires the disclosure of information regarding the beneficial owner of an interest in a person.

Paragraph 6 of Article XXVII

The substance of new paragraph 6 is similar to the second sentence of paragraph 2 of Article XXVII of the existing Convention. New paragraph 6 adopts the language of paragraph 6 of Article 26 (Exchange of Information and Administrative Assistance) of the U.S. Model. New paragraph 6 provides that the requesting State may specify the form in which information is to be provided (*e.g.*, depositions of witnesses and authenticated copies of original documents). The intention is to ensure that the information may be introduced as evidence in the judicial proceedings of the requesting State.

The requested State should, if possible, provide the information in the form requested to the same extent that it can obtain information in that form under its own laws and administrative practices with respect to its own taxes.

Paragraph 7 of Article XXVII

New paragraph 7 is consistent with paragraph 8 of Article 26 (Exchange of Information and Administrative Assistance) of the U.S. Model. Paragraph 7 provides that the requested State shall allow representatives of the requesting State to enter the requested State to interview individuals and examine books and records with the consent of the persons subject to examination. Paragraph 7 was intended to reinforce that the administrations can conduct consensual tax examinations abroad, and was not intended to limit travel or supersede any arrangements or procedures the competent authorities may have previously had in place regarding travel for tax administration purposes.

Paragraph 13 of General Note

As is explained in paragraph 13 of the General Note, the United States and Canada understand and agree that the standards and practices described in Article XXVII of the Convention are to be in no respect less effective than those described in the Model Agreement on Exchange of Information on Tax Matters developed by the OECD Global Forum Working Group on Effective Exchange of Information.

Article 24

Article 24 amends Article XXIX (Miscellaneous Rules) of the Convention.

Paragraph 1

Paragraph 1 replaces paragraph 2 of Article XXIX of the existing Convention. New paragraph 2 is divided into two subparagraphs. In general, subparagraph 2(a) provides a "saving clause" pursuant to which the United States and Canada may each tax its residents, as determined under Article IV (Residence), and the United States may tax its citizens and companies, including those electing to be treated as domestic corporations (*e.g.* under Code section 1504(d)), as if there were no convention between the United States and Canada with respect to taxes on income and capital. Subparagraph 2(a) contains language that generally corresponds to former paragraph 2, but omits certain language pertaining to former citizens, which are addressed in new subparagraph 2(b).

New subparagraph 2(b) generally corresponds to the provisions of former paragraph 2 addressing former citizens of the United States. However, new subparagraph 2(b) also includes a reference to former long-term residents of the United States. This addition, as well as other changes in subparagraph 2(b), brings the Convention in conformity with the U.S. taxation of former citizens and long-term residents under Code section 877.

Similar to subparagraph 2(a), new subparagraph 2(b) operates as a "saving clause" and provides that notwithstanding the other provisions of the Convention, a former citizen or former long-term resident of the United States, may, for a period of ten years following the loss of such status, be taxed in accordance with the laws of the United States with respect to income from sources within the United States (including income deemed under the domestic law of the United States to arise from such sources).

Paragraphs 11 and 12 of the General Note provide definitions based on Code section 877 that are relevant to the application of paragraph 2 of Article XXIX. Paragraph 11 of the General Note provides that the term "long-term resident" means any individual who is a lawful permanent resident of the United States in eight or more taxable years during the preceding 15 taxable years. In determining whether the eight-year threshold is met, one does not count any year in which the individual is treated as a resident of Canada under this Convention (or as a resident of any country other than the United States under the provisions of any other U.S. tax treaty), and the individual does not waive the benefits of such treaty applicable to residents of the other country. This understanding is consistent with how this provision is generally interpreted in U.S. tax treaties.

Paragraph 12 of the General Note provides that the phrase "income deemed under the domestic law of the United States to arise from such sources" as used in new subparagraph 2(b) includes gains from the sale or exchange of stock of a U.S. company or debt obligations of a U.S. person, the United States, a State, or a political subdivision thereof, or the District of Columbia, gains from property (other than stock or debt obligations) located in the United States, and, in certain cases, income or gain derived from the sale of stock of a non-U.S. company or a disposition of property contributed to such non-U.S. company where such company would be a controlled foreign corporation with respect to the individual if such person had continued to be a U.S. person. In addition, an individual who exchanges property that gives rise or would give rise to U.S.-source income for property that gives rise to foreign-source income will be treated as if he had sold the property that would give rise to U.S.-source income for its fair market value, and any consequent gain shall be deemed to be income from sources within the United States.

Paragraph 2

Paragraph 2 replaces subparagraph 3(a) of Article XXIX of the existing Convention. Paragraph 3 provides that, notwithstanding paragraph 2 of Article XXIX, the United States and Canada must respect specified provisions of the Convention in regard to certain persons, including residents and citizens. Therefore, subparagraph 3(a) lists certain paragraphs and Articles of the Convention that represent exceptions to the "saving clause" in all situations. New subparagraph 3(a) is substantially similar to former subparagraph 3(a), but now contains a reference to paragraphs 8, 10, and 13 of Article XVIII (Pensions and Annuities) to reflect the changes made to that article in paragraph 3 of Article 13 of the Protocol.

Article 25

Article 25 of the Protocol replaces Article XXIX A (Limitation on Benefits) of the existing Convention, which was added to the Convention by the Protocol done on March 17, 1995. Article XXIX A addresses the problem of "treaty shopping" by residents of third States by requiring, in most cases, that the person seeking benefits not only be a U.S. resident or Canadian resident but also satisfy other tests. For example, a resident of a third State might establish an entity resident in Canada for the purpose of deriving income from the United States and claiming U.S. treaty benefits with respect to that income. Article XXIX A limits the benefits granted by the United States or Canada under the Convention to those persons whose residence in the other Contracting State is not considered to have been motivated by the existence of the Convention. As replaced by the Protocol, new Article XXIX A is reciprocal, and many of the changes to the former paragraphs of Article XXIX A are made to effectuate this reciprocal application.

Absent Article XXIX A, an entity resident in one of the Contracting States would be entitled to benefits under the Convention, unless it were denied such benefits as a result of limitations under domestic law (*e.g.*, business purpose, substance-over-form, step transaction, or conduit principles or other anti-avoidance rules) applicable to a particular transaction or arrangement. As noted below in the explanation of paragraph 7, general anti-abuse provisions of this sort apply in conjunction with the Convention in both the United States and Canada. In the case of the United States, such anti-abuse provisions complement the explicit anti-treaty-shopping rules of Article XXIX A. While the anti-treaty-shopping rules determine whether a person has a sufficient nexus to Canada to be entitled to benefits under the Convention, the anti-abuse provisions under U.S. domestic law determine whether a particular transaction should be recast in accordance with the substance of the transaction.

Paragraph 1 of Article XXIX A

New paragraph 1 of Article XXIX A provides that, for the purposes of the application of the Convention, a "qualifying person" shall be entitled to all of the benefits of the Convention and, except as provided in paragraphs 3, 4, and 6, a person that is not a qualifying person shall not be entitled to any benefits of the Convention.

Paragraph 2 of Article XXIX A

New paragraph 2 lists a number of characteristics any one of which will make a United States or Canadian resident a qualifying person. The "look-through" principles introduced by the Protocol (e.g. paragraph 6 of Article IV (Residence)) are to be applied in conjunction with Article XXIX A. Accordingly, the provisions of Article IV shall determine the person who derives an item of income, and the objective tests of Article XXIX A shall be applied to that person to determine whether benefits shall be granted. The rules are essentially mechanical tests and are discussed below.

Individuals and governmental entities

Under new paragraph 2, the first two categories of qualifying persons are (1) natural persons resident in the United States or Canada (as listed in subparagraph 2(a)), and (2) the Contracting States, political subdivisions or local authorities thereof, and any agency or instrumentality of such Government, political subdivision or local authority (as listed in subparagraph 2(b)). Persons falling into these two categories are unlikely to be used, as the beneficial owner of income, to derive benefits under the Convention on behalf of a third-country person. If such a person receives income as a nominee on behalf of a third-country resident, benefits will be denied with respect to those items of income under the articles of the Convention that would otherwise grant the benefit, because of the requirements in those articles that the beneficial owner of the income be a resident of a Contracting State.

Publicly traded entities

Under new subparagraph 2(c), a company or trust resident in a Contracting State is a qualifying person if the company's principal class of shares, and any disproportionate class of shares, or the trust's units, or disproportionate interest in a trust, are primarily and regularly traded on one or more recognized stock exchanges. The term "recognized stock exchange" is defined in subparagraph 5(f) of the Article to mean, in the United States, the NASDAQ System and any stock exchange registered as a national securities exchange with the Securities and Exchange Commission, and, in Canada, any Canadian stock exchanges that are "prescribed stock exchanges" or "designated stock exchanges" under the Income Tax Act. These are, at the time of signature of the Protocol, the Montreal Stock Exchange, the Toronto Stock Exchange, and Tiers 1 and 2 of the TSX Venture Exchange. Additional exchanges may be added to the list of recognized exchanges by exchange of notes between the Contracting States or by agreement between the competent authorities.

If a company has only one class of shares, it is only necessary to consider whether the shares of that class meet the relevant trading requirements. If the company has more than one class of shares, it is necessary as an initial matter to determine which class or classes constitute the "principal class of shares." The term "principal class of shares" is defined in subparagraph 5(e) of the Article to mean the ordinary or common shares of the company representing the majority of the aggregate voting power and value of the company. If the company does not have a class of ordinary or common shares representing the majority of the aggregate voting power and value of the company, then the "principal class of shares" is that class or any combination of classes of shares that represents, in the aggregate, a majority of the voting power and value of the company. Although in a particular case involving a company with several classes of shares it is conceivable that more than one group of classes could be identified that account for more than 50% of the voting power and value of the shares of the company, it is only necessary for one such group to satisfy the requirements of this subparagraph in order for the company to be entitled to benefits. Benefits would not be denied to the company even if a second, non-qualifying, group of shares with more than half of the company's voting power and value could be identified.

A company whose principal class of shares is regularly traded on a recognized stock exchange will nevertheless not qualify for benefits under subparagraph 2(c) if it has a disproportionate class of shares that is not regularly traded on a recognized stock exchange. The term "disproportionate class of shares" is defined in subparagraph 5(b) of the Article. A company has a disproportionate class of shares if it has outstanding a class of shares which is subject to terms or other arrangements that entitle the holder to a larger portion of the company's income, profit, or gain in the other Contracting State than that to which the holder would be entitled in the absence of such terms or arrangements. Thus, for example, a company has a disproportionate class of shares if it has outstanding a class of "tracking stock" that pays dividends based upon a formula that approximates the company's return on its assets employed in the United States. Similar principles apply to determine whether or not there are disproportionate interests in a trust.

The following example illustrates the application of subparagraph 5(b).

Example. OCo is a corporation resident in Canada. OCo has two classes of shares: Common and Preferred. The Common shares are listed and regularly traded on a designated stock exchange in Canada. The Preferred shares have no voting rights and are entitled to receive dividends equal in amount to interest payments that OCo receives from unrelated borrowers in the United States. The Preferred shares are owned entirely by a single investor that is a resident of a country with which the United States does not have a tax treaty. The Common shares account for more than 50 percent of the value of OCo and for 100 percent of the voting power. Because the owner of the Preferred shares is entitled to receive payments corresponding to the U.S.-source interest income earned by OCo, the Preferred shares are a disproportionate class of shares. Because the Preferred shares are not primarily and regularly traded on a recognized stock exchange, OCo will not qualify for benefits under subparagraph 2(c).

The term "regularly traded" is not defined in the Convention. In accordance with paragraph 2 of Article III (General Definitions) and paragraph 1 of the General Note, this term will be defined by reference to the domestic tax laws of the State from which benefits of the Convention are sought, generally the source State. In the case of the United States, this term is understood to have the meaning it has under Treas. Reg. section 1.884-5(d)(4)(i)(B), relating to the branch tax provisions of the Code, as may be amended from time to time. Under these regulations, a class of shares is considered to be "regularly traded" if two requirements are met: trades in the class of shares are made in more than de minimis quantities on at least 60 days during the taxable year, and the aggregate number of shares in the class traded during the year is at least 10 percent of the average number of shares outstanding during the year. Sections 1.884-5(d)(4)(i)(A), (ii) and (iii) will not be taken into account for purposes of defining the term "regularly traded" under the Convention.

The regularly-traded requirement can be met by trading on one or more recognized stock exchanges. Therefore, trading may be aggregated for purposes of this requirement. Thus, a U.S. company could satisfy the regularly traded requirement through trading, in whole or in part, on a recognized stock exchange located in Canada. Authorized but unissued shares are not considered for purposes of this test.

The term "primarily traded" is not defined in the Convention. In accordance with paragraph 2 of Article III (General Definitions) and paragraph 1 of the General Note, this term will have the meaning it has under the laws of the State concerning the taxes to which the Convention applies, generally the source State. In the case of the United States, this term is understood to have the meaning it has under Treas. Reg. section 1.884-5(d)(3), as may be amended from time to time, relating to the branch tax provisions of the Code. Accordingly, stock of a corporation is "primarily traded" if the number of shares in the company's principal class of shares that are traded during the taxable year on all recognized stock exchanges exceeds the number of shares in the company's principal class of shares that are traded during that year on all other established securities markets.

Subject to the adoption by Canada of other definitions, the U.S. interpretation of "regularly traded" and "primarily traded" will be considered to apply, with such modifications as circumstances require, under the Convention for purposes of Canadian taxation.

Subsidiaries of publicly traded entities

Certain companies owned by publicly traded corporations also may be qualifying persons. Under subparagraph 2(d), a company resident in the United States or Canada will be a qualifying person, even if not publicly traded, if more than 50 percent of the vote and value of its shares, and more than 50 percent of the vote and value of each disproportionate class of shares, is owned (directly or indirectly) by five or fewer persons that are qualifying persons under subparagraph 2(c). In addition, each company in the chain of ownership must be a qualifying person. Thus, for example, a company that is a resident of Canada, all the shares of which are owned by another company that is a resident of Canada, would qualify for benefits of the Convention if the principal class of shares (and any disproportionate classes of shares) of the parent company are regularly and primarily traded on a recognized stock exchange. However, such a subsidiary would not qualify for benefits under subparagraph 2(d) if the publicly traded parent company were a resident of a third state, for example, and not a resident of the United States or Canada. Furthermore, if a parent company qualifying for benefits under subparagraph 2(c) indirectly owned the bottom-tier company through a chain of subsidiaries, each subsidiary in the chain, as an intermediate owner, must be a qualifying person in order for the bottom-tier subsidiary to meet the test in subparagraph 2(d).

Subparagraph 2(d) provides that a subsidiary can take into account ownership by as many as five companies, each of which qualifies for benefits under subparagraph 2(c) to determine if the subsidiary qualifies for benefits under subparagraph 2(d). For example, a Canadian company that is not publicly traded but that is owned, one-third each, by three companies, two of which are Canadian resident corporations whose principal classes of shares are primarily and regularly traded on a recognized stock exchange, will qualify under subparagraph 2(d).

By applying the principles introduced by the Protocol (e.g. paragraph 6 of Article IV) in the context of this rule, one "looks through" entities in the chain of ownership that are viewed as fiscally transparent under the domestic laws of the State of residence (other than entities that are resident in the State of source).

The 50-percent test under subparagraph 2(d) applies only to shares other than "debt substitute shares." The term "debt substitute shares" is defined in subparagraph 5(a) to mean shares defined in paragraph (e) of the definition in the Canadian Income Tax Act of "term preferred shares" (see subsection 248(1) of the Income Tax Act), which relates to certain shares received in debt-restructuring arrangements undertaken by reason of financial difficulty or insolvency. Subparagraph 5(a) also provides that the competent authorities may agree to treat other types of shares as debt substitute shares.

Ownership/base erosion test

Subparagraph 2(e) provides a two-part test under which certain other entities may be qualifying persons, based on ownership and lack of "base erosion." A company resident in the United States or Canada will satisfy the first of these tests if 50 percent or more of the vote and value of its shares and 50 percent or more of the vote and value of each disproportionate class of shares, in both cases not including debt substitute shares, is not owned, directly or indirectly, by persons other than qualifying persons. Similarly, a trust resident in the United States or Canada will satisfy this first test if 50 percent or more of its beneficial interests, and 50 percent or more of each disproportionate interest, is not owned, directly or indirectly, by persons other than qualifying persons. The wording of these tests is intended to make clear that, for example, if a Canadian company is more than 50 percent owned, either directly or indirectly (including cumulative indirect ownership through a chain of entities), by a U.S. resident corporation that is, itself, wholly owned by a third-country resident other than a qualifying person, the Canadian company would not pass the ownership test. This is because more than 50 percent of its shares is owned indirectly by a person (the third-country resident) that is not a qualifying person.

It is understood by the Contracting States that in determining whether a company satisfies the ownership test described in subparagraph 2(e)(i), a company, 50 percent of more of the aggregate vote and value of the shares of which and 50 percent or more of the vote and value of each disproportionate class of shares (in neither case including debt substitute shares) of which is owned, directly or indirectly, by a company described in subparagraph 2(c) will satisfy the ownership test of subparagraph 2(e)(i). In such case, no further analysis of the ownership of the company described in subparagraph 2(c) is required. Similarly, in determining whether a trust satisfies the ownership test described in subparagraph 2(e)(ii), a trust, 50 percent or more of the beneficial interest in which and 50 percent or more of each disproportionate interest in which, is owned, directly or indirectly, by a trust described in subparagraph (2)(c) will satisfy the ownership test of subparagraph (2)(e)(ii), and no further analysis of the ownership of the trust described in subparagraph 2(c) is required.

The second test of subparagraph 2(e) is the so-called "base erosion" test. A company or trust that passes the ownership test must also pass this test to be a qualifying person under this subparagraph. This test requires that the amount of expenses that are paid or payable by the entity in question, directly or indirectly, to persons that are not qualifying persons, and that are deductible from gross income (with both deductibility and gross income as determined under the tax laws of the State of residence of the company or trust), be less than 50 percent of the gross income of the company or trust. This test is applied for the fiscal period immediately preceding the period for which the qualifying person test is being applied. If it is the first fiscal period of the person, the test is applied for the current period.

The ownership/base erosion test recognizes that the benefits of the Convention can be enjoyed indirectly not only by equity holders of an entity, but also by that entity's obligees, such as lenders, licensors, service providers, insurers and reinsurers, and others. For example, a third-country resident could license technology to a Canadian-owned Canadian corporation to be sub-licensed to a U.S. resident. The U.S.-source royalty income of the Canadian corporation would be exempt from U.S. withholding tax under Article XII (Royalties) of the Convention. While the Canadian corporation would be subject to Canadian corporation income tax, its taxable income could be reduced to near zero as a result of the deductible royalties paid to the third-country resident. If, under a convention between Canada and the third country, those royalties were either exempt from Canadian tax or subject to tax at a low rate, the U.S. treaty benefit with respect to the U.S.-source royalty income would have flowed to the third-country resident at little or no tax cost, with no reciprocal benefit to the United States from the third country. The ownership/base erosion test therefore requires both that qualifying persons substantially own the entity and that the entity's tax base is not substantially eroded by payments (directly or indirectly) to nonqualifying persons.

For purposes of this subparagraph 2(e) and other provisions of this Article, the term "shares" includes, in the case of a mutual insurance company, any certificate or contract entitling the holder to voting power in the corporation. This is consistent with the interpretation of similar limitation on benefits provisions in other U.S. treaties. In Canada, the principles that are reflected in subsection 256(8.1) of the Income Tax Act will be applied, in effect treating memberships, policies or other interests in a corporation incorporated without share capital as representing an appropriate number of shares.

The look-through principles introduced by the Protocol (e.g. new paragraph 6 of Article IV) are to be taken into account when applying the ownership and base erosion provisions of Article XXIX A. Therefore, one "looks through" an entity that is viewed as fiscally transparent under the domestic laws of the residence State (other than entities that are resident in the source State) when applying the ownership/base erosion test. Assume, for example, that USCo, a company incorporated in the United States, wishes to obtain treaty benefits by virtue of the ownership and base erosion rule. USCo is owned by USLLC, an entity that is treated as fiscally transparent in the United States. USLLC in turn is wholly owned in equal shares by 10 individuals who are residents of the United States. Because the United States views USLLC as fiscally transparent, the 10 U.S. individuals shall be regarded as the owners of USCo for purposes of the ownership test. Accordingly, USCo would satisfy the ownership requirement of the ownership/base erosion test. However, if USLLC were instead owned in equal shares by four U.S. individuals and six individuals who are not residents of either the United States or

56

Canada, USCo would not satisfy the ownership requirement. Similarly, for purposes of the base erosion test, deductible payments made to USLLC will be treated as made to USLLC's owners.

Other qualifying persons

Under new subparagraph 2(f), an estate resident in the United States or Canada is a qualifying person entitled to the benefits of the Convention.

New subparagraphs 2(g) and 2(h) specify the circumstances under which certain types of not-for-profit organizations will be qualifying persons. Subparagraph 2(g) provides that a not-for-profit organization that is resident in the United States or Canada is a qualifying person, and thus entitled to benefits, if more than half of the beneficiaries, members, or participants in the organization are qualifying persons. The term "not-for-profit organization" of a Contracting State is defined in subparagraph 5(d) of the Article to mean an entity created or established in that State that is generally exempt from income taxation in that State by reason of its not-for-profit status. The term includes charities, private foundations, trade unions, trade associations, and similar organizations.

New subparagraph 2(h) specifies that certain trusts, companies, organizations, or other arrangements described in paragraph 2 of Article XXI (Exempt Organizations) are qualifying persons. To be a qualifying person, the trust, company, organization or other arrangement must be established for the purpose of providing pension, retirement, or employee benefits primarily to individuals who are (or were, within any of the five preceding years) qualifying persons. A trust, company, organization, or other arrangement will be considered to be established for the purpose of providing benefits primarily to such persons if more than 50 percent of its beneficiaries, members, or participants are such persons. Thus, for example, a Canadian Registered Retirement Savings Plan ("RRSP") of a former resident of Canada who is working temporarily outside of Canada would continue to be a qualifying person during the period of the individual's absence from Canada or for five years, whichever is shorter. A Canadian pension fund established to provide benefits to persons employed by a company would be a qualifying person only if most of the beneficiaries of the fund are (or were within the five preceding years) individual residents of Canada or residents or citizens of the United States.

New subparagraph 2(i) specifies that certain trusts, companies, organizations, or other arrangements described in paragraph 3 of Article XXI (Exempt Organizations) are qualifying persons. To be a qualifying person, the beneficiaries of a trust, company, organization or other arrangement must be described in subparagraph 2(g) or 2(h).

The provisions of paragraph 2 are self-executing, unlike the provisions of paragraph 6, discussed below. The tax authorities may, of course, on review, determine that the taxpayer has improperly interpreted the paragraph and is not entitled to the benefits claimed.

Paragraph 3 of Article XXIX A

Paragraph 3 provides an alternative rule, under which a United States or Canadian resident that is not a qualifying person under paragraph 2 may claim benefits with respect to those items of income that are connected with the active conduct of a trade or business in its State of residence.

This is the so-called "active trade or business" test. Unlike the tests of paragraph 2, the active trade or business test looks not solely at the characteristics of the person deriving the income, but also at the nature of the person's activity and the connection between the income and that activity. Under the active trade or business test, a resident of a Contracting State deriving an item of income from the other Contracting State is entitled to benefits with respect to that income if that person (or a person related to that person under the principles of Code section 482, or in the case of Canada, section 251 of the Income Tax Act) is engaged in an active trade or business in the State where it is resident, the income in question is derived in connection with, or is incidental to, that trade or business, and the size of the active trade or business in the residence State is substantial relative to the activity in the other State that gives rise to the income for which benefits are sought. Further details on the application of the substantiality requirement are provided below.

Income that is derived in connection with, or is incidental to, the business of making or managing investments will not qualify for benefits under this provision, unless those investment activities are carried on with customers in the ordinary course of the business of a bank, insurance company, registered securities dealer, or deposit-taking financial institution.

Income is considered derived "in connection" with an active trade or business if, for example, the income-generating activity in the State is "upstream," "downstream," or parallel to that conducted in the other Contracting State. Thus, for example, if the U.S. activity of a Canadian resident company consisted of selling the output of a Canadian manufacturer or providing inputs to the manufacturing process, or of manufacturing or selling in the United States the same sorts of products that were being sold by the Canadian trade or business in Canada, the income generated by that activity would be treated as earned in connection with the Canadian trade or business. Income is considered "incidental" to a trade or business if, for example, it arises from the short-term investment of working capital of the resident in securities issued by persons in the State of source.

An item of income may be considered to be earned in connection with or to be incidental to an active trade or business in the United States or Canada even though the resident claiming the benefits derives the income directly or indirectly through one or more other persons that are residents of the other Contracting State. Thus, for example, a Canadian resident could claim benefits with respect to an item of income earned by a U.S. operating subsidiary but derived by the Canadian resident indirectly through a wholly-owned U.S. holding company interposed between it and the operating subsidiary. This language would also permit a resident to derive income from the other Contracting State through one or more residents of that other State that it does not wholly own. For example, a Canadian partnership in which three unrelated Canadian companies each hold a one-third interest could form a wholly-owned U.S. holding company with a U.S. operating subsidiary. The "directly or indirectly" language would allow otherwise unavailable treaty benefits to be claimed with respect to income derived by the three Canadian partners through the U.S. holding company, even if the partners were not considered to be related to the U.S. holding company under the principles of Code section 482.

As described above, income that is derived in connection with, or is incidental to, an active trade or business in a Contracting State, must pass the substantiality requirement to qualify for benefits under the Convention. The trade or business must be substantial in relation to the activity in the other Contracting State that gave rise to the income in respect of which benefits under the Convention are being claimed. To be considered substantial, it is not necessary that the trade or business be as large as the income-generating activity. The trade or business cannot, however, in terms of income, assets, or other similar measures, represent only a very small percentage of the size of the activity in the other State.

The substantiality requirement is intended to prevent treaty shopping. For example, a third-country resident may want to acquire a U.S. company that manufactures television sets for worldwide markets; however, since its country of residence has no tax treaty with the United States, any dividends generated by the investment would be subject to a U.S. withholding tax of 30 percent. Absent a substantiality test, the investor could establish a Canadian corporation that would operate a small outlet in Canada to sell a few of the television sets manufactured by the U.S. company and earn a very small amount of income. That Canadian corporation could then acquire the U.S. manufacturer with capital provided by the third-country resident and produce a very large number of sets for sale in several countries, generating a much larger amount of income. It might attempt to argue that the U.S.-source income is generated from business activities in the United States related to the television sales activity of the Canadian parent and that the dividend income should be subject to U.S. tax at the 5 percent rate provided by Article X (Dividends) of the Convention. However, the substantiality test would not be met in this example, so the dividends would remain subject to withholding in the United States at a rate of 30 percent.

It is expected that if a person qualifies for benefits under one of the tests of paragraph 2, no inquiry will be made into qualification for benefits under paragraph 3. Upon satisfaction of any of the tests of paragraph 2, any income derived by the beneficial owner from the other Contracting State is entitled to treaty benefits. Under paragraph 3, however, the test is applied separately to each item of income.

Paragraph 4 of Article XXIX A

Paragraph 4 provides a limited "derivative benefits" test that entitles a company that is a resident of the United States or Canada to the benefits of Articles X (Dividends), XI (Interest), and XII (Royalties), even if the company is not a qualifying person and does not satisfy the active trade or business test of paragraph 3. In general, a derivative benefits test entitles the resident of a Contracting State to treaty benefits if the owner of the resident would have been entitled to the same benefit had the income in question been earned directly by that owner. To qualify under this paragraph, the company must satisfy both the ownership test in subparagraph 4(a) and the base erosion test of subparagraph 4(b).

Under subparagraph 4(a), the derivative benefits ownership test requires that the company's shares representing more than 90 percent of the aggregate vote and value of all of the shares of the company, and at least 50 percent of the vote and value of any disproportionate class of shares, in neither case including debt substitute shares, be owned directly or indirectly by persons each of whom is either (i) a qualifying person or (ii) another person that satisfies each of three tests. The three tests of subparagraph 4(a) that must be satisfied by these other persons are as follows:

First, the other person must be a resident of a third State with which the Contracting State that is granting benefits has a comprehensive income tax convention. The other person must be entitled to all of the benefits under that convention. Thus, if the person fails to satisfy the limitation on benefits tests, if any, of that convention, no benefits would be granted under this paragraph. Qualification for benefits under an active trade or business test does not suffice for these purposes, because that test grants benefits only for certain items of income, not for all purposes of the convention.

Second, the other person must be a person that would qualify for benefits with respect to the item of income for which benefits are sought under one or more of the tests of paragraph 2 or 3 of Article XXIX A, if the person were a resident of the Contracting State that is not providing benefits for the item of income and, for purposes of paragraph 3, the business were carried on in that State. For example, a person resident in a third country would be deemed to be a person that would qualify under the publicly-traded test of paragraph 2 of Article XXIX A if the principal class of its shares were primarily and regularly traded on a stock exchange recognized either under the Convention between the United States and Canada or under the treaty between the Contracting State granting benefits and the third country. Similarly, a company resident in a third country would be deemed to satisfy the ownership/base erosion test of paragraph 2 under this hypothetical analysis if, for example, it were wholly owned by an individual resident in that third country and the company's tax base were not substantially eroded by payments (directly or indirectly) to nonqualifying persons.

The third requirement is that the rate of tax on the item of income in respect of which benefits are sought must be at least as low under the convention between the person's country of residence and the Contracting State granting benefits as it is under the Convention.

Subparagraph 4(b) sets forth the base erosion test. This test requires that the amount of expenses that are paid or payable by the company in question, directly or indirectly, to persons that are not qualifying persons under the Convention, and that are deductible from gross income (with both deductibility and gross income as determined under the tax laws of the State of residence of the company), be less than 50 percent of the gross income of the company. This test is applied for the fiscal period immediately preceding the period for which the test is being applied. If it is the first fiscal period of the person, the test is applied for the current period. This test is qualitatively the same as the base erosion test of subparagraph 2(e).

Paragraph 5 of Article XXIX A

Paragraph 5 defines certain terms used in the Article. These terms were identified and discussed in connection with new paragraph 2, above.

Paragraph 6 of Article XXIX A

Paragraph 6 provides that when a resident of a Contracting State derives income from the other Contracting State and is not entitled to the benefits of the Convention under other provisions of the Article, benefits may, nevertheless be granted at the discretion of the competent authority of the other Contracting State. This determination can be made with respect to all benefits under the Convention or on an item by item basis. In making a determination under this paragraph, the competent authority will take into account all relevant facts and circumstances relating to the person requesting the benefits. In particular, the competent authority will consider the history, structure, ownership (including ultimate beneficial ownership), and operations of the person. In addition, the competent authority is to consider (1) whether the creation and existence of the person did not have as a principal purpose obtaining treaty benefits that would not otherwise be available to the person, and (2) whether it would not be appropriate, in view of the purpose of the Article, to deny benefits. If the competent authority of the other

Contracting State determines that either of these two standards is satisfied, benefits shall be granted.

For purposes of implementing new paragraph 6, a taxpayer will be permitted to present his case to the competent authority for an advance determination based on a full disclosure of all pertinent information. The taxpayer will not be required to wait until it has been determined that benefits are denied under one of the other provisions of the Article. It also is expected that, if and when the competent authority determines that benefits are to be allowed, they will be allowed retroactively to the time of entry into force of the relevant provision of the Convention or the establishment of the structure in question, whichever is later (assuming that the taxpayer also qualifies under the relevant facts for the earlier period).

Paragraph 7 of Article XXIX A

New paragraph 7 is in substance similar to paragraph 7 of Article XXIX A of the existing Convention and clarifies the application of general anti-abuse provisions. New paragraph 7 provides that paragraphs 1 through 6 of Article XXIX A shall not be construed as limiting in any manner the right of a Contracting State to deny benefits under the Convention where it can reasonably be concluded that to do otherwise would result in an abuse of the provisions of the Convention. This provision permits a Contracting State to rely on general anti-avoidance rules to counter arrangements involving treaty shopping through the other Contracting State.

Thus, Canada may apply its domestic law rules to counter abusive arrangements involving "treaty shopping" through the United States, and the United States may apply its substance-over-form and anti-conduit rules, for example, in relation to Canadian residents. This principle is recognized by the OECD in the Commentaries to its Model Tax Convention on Income and on Capital, and the United States and Canada agree that it is inherent in the Convention. The statement of this principle explicitly in the Protocol is not intended to suggest that the principle is not also inherent in other tax conventions concluded by the United States or Canada.

Article 26

Article 26 of the Protocol replaces paragraphs 1 and 5 of Article XXIX B (Taxes Imposed by Reason of Death) of the Convention. In addition, paragraph 7 of the General Note provides certain clarifications for purposes of paragraphs 6 and 7 of Article XXIX B.

Paragraph 1

Paragraph 1 of Article XXIX B of the existing Convention generally addresses the situation where a resident of a Contracting State passes property by reason of the individual's death to an organization referred to in paragraph 1 of Article XXI (Exempt Organizations) of the Convention. The paragraph provided that the tax consequences in a Contracting State arising out of the passing of the property shall apply as if the organization were a resident of that State.

The Protocol replaces paragraph 1, and the changes set forth in new paragraph 1 are intended to specifically address questions that have arisen about the application of former paragraph 1 where property of an individual who is a resident of Canada passes by reason of the individual's death to a charitable organization in the United States that is not a "registered charity" under Canadian law. Under one view, paragraph 1 of Article

61

XXIX B requires Canada to treat the passing of the property as a contribution to a "registered charity" and thus to allow all of the same deductions for Canadian tax purposes as if the U.S. charity had been a "registered charity" under Canadian law. Under another view, paragraph 6 of Article XXI (Exempt Organizations) of the Convention continues to limit the amount of the income tax charitable deduction in Canada to the individual's income arising in the United States. The changes set forth in new paragraph 1 are intended to provide relief from the Canadian tax on gain deemed recognized by reason of death that would otherwise give rise to Canadian tax when the individual passes the property to a charitable organization in the United States, but, for purposes of the separate Canadian income tax, do not eliminate the limitation under paragraph 6 of Article XXI on the amount of the deduction in Canada for the charitable donation to the individual's income arising in the United States.

As revised, paragraph 1 is divided into two subparagraphs. New subparagraph 1(a) applies where property of an individual who is a resident of the United States passes by reason of the individual's death to a qualifying exempt organization that is a resident of Canada. In such case, the tax consequences in the United States arising from the passing of such property apply as if the organization were a resident of the United States. A bequest by a U.S. citizen or U.S. resident (as defined for estate tax purposes under the Code) to an exempt organization generally is deductible for U.S. federal estate tax purposes under Code section 2055, without regard to whether the organization is a U.S. corporation. Thus, generally, the individual's estate will be entitled to a charitable deduction for Federal estate tax purposes equal to the value of the property transferred to the organization. Generally, the effect is that no Federal estate tax will be imposed on the value of the property.

New subparagraph 1(b) applies where property of an individual who is a resident of Canada passes by reason of the individual's death to a qualifying exempt organization that is a resident of the United States. In such case, for purposes of the Canadian capital gains tax imposed at death, the tax consequences arising out of the passing of the property shall apply as if the individual disposed of the property for proceeds equal to an amount elected on behalf of the individual. For this purpose, the amount elected shall be no less than the individual's cost of the property as determined for purposes of Canadian tax, and no greater than the fair market value of the property. The manner in which the individual's representative shall make this election shall be specified by the competent authority of Canada. Generally, in the event of a full exercise of the election under new subparagraph 1(b), no capital gains tax will be imposed in Canada by reason of the death with regard to that property.

New paragraph 1 does not address the situation in which a resident of one Contracting State bequeaths property with a situs in the other Contracting State to a qualifying exempt organization in the Contracting State of the decedent's residence. In such a situation, the other Contracting State may impose tax by reason of death, for example, if the property is real property situated in that State.

Paragraph 2

Paragraph 2 of Article 26 of the Protocol replaces paragraph 5 of Article XXIX B of the existing Convention. The provisions of new paragraph 5 relate to the operation of Canadian law. Because Canadian law requires both spouses to have been Canadian residents in order to be eligible for the rollover, these provisions are intended to provide deferral ("rollover") of the Canadian tax at death for certain transfers to a surviving spouse and to permit the Canadian competent authority to allow such deferral for certain transfers to a trust. For example, they would enable the competent authority to treat a trust that is a qualified domestic trust for U.S. estate tax purposes as a Canadian spousal trust as well for purposes of certain provisions of Canadian tax law and of the Convention. These provisions do not affect U.S. domestic law regarding qualified domestic trusts. Nor do they affect the status of U.S. resident individuals for any other purpose.

New paragraph 5 adds a reference to subsection 70(5.2) of the Canadian Income Tax Act. This change is needed because the rollover in respect of certain kinds of property is provided in that subsection. Further, new paragraph 5 adds a clause "and with respect to such property" near the end of the second sentence to make it clear that the trust is treated as a resident of Canada only with respect to its Canadian property.

For example, assume that a U.S. decedent with a Canadian spouse sets up a qualified domestic trust holding U.S. and Canadian real property, and that the decedent's executor elects, for Federal estate tax purposes, to treat the entire trust as qualifying for the Federal estate tax marital deduction. Under Canadian law, because the decedent is not a Canadian resident, Canada would impose capital gains tax on the deemed disposition of the Canadian real property immediately before death. In order to defer the Canadian tax that might otherwise be imposed by reason of the decedent's death, under new paragraph 5 of Article XXIX B, the competent authority of Canada shall, at the request of the trustee, treat the trust as a Canadian spousal trust with respect to the Canadian real property. The effect of such treatment is to defer the tax on the deemed distribution of the Canadian real property until an appropriate triggering event such as the death of the surviving spouse.

Paragraph 7 of the General Note

In addition to the foregoing, paragraph 7 of the General Note provides certain clarifications for purposes of paragraphs 6 and 7 of Article XXIX B. These clarifications ensure that tax credits will be available in cases where there are inconsistencies in the way the two Contracting States view the income and the property.

Subparagraph 7(a) of the General Note applies where an individual who immediately before death was a resident of Canada held at the time of death a share or option in respect of a share that constitutes property situated in the United States for the purposes of Article XXIX B and that Canada views as giving rise to employment income (for example, a share or option granted by an employer). The United States imposes estate tax on the share or option in respect of a share, while Canada imposes income tax on income from employment. Subparagraph 7(a) provides that for purposes of clause 6(a)(ii) of Article XXIX B, any employment income in respect of the share or option constitutes income from property situated in the United States. This provision ensures that the estate tax paid on the share or option in the United States will be allowable as a deduction from the Canadian income tax.

Subparagraph 7(b) of the General Note applies where an individual who immediately before death was a resident of Canada held at the time of death a registered retirement savings plan (RRSP) or other entity that is a resident of Canada and that is described in subparagraph 1(b) of Article IV (Residence) and such RRSP or other entity held property situated in the United States for the purposes of Article XXIX B. The United States would impose estate tax on the value of the property held by the RRSP or other entity (to the extent such property is subject to Federal estate tax), while Canada would impose income tax on a deemed distribution of the property in the RRSP or other entity. Subparagraph 7(b) provides that any income out of or under the entity in respect of the property is, for the purpose of subparagraph 6(a)(ii) of Article XXIX B, income from property situated in the United States. This provision ensures that the estate tax paid on the underlying property in the United States (if any) will be allowable as a deduction from the Canadian income tax.

Subparagraph 7(c) of the General Note applies where an individual who immediately before death was a resident or citizen of the United States held at the time of death an RRSP or other entity that is a resident of Canada and that is described in subparagraph 1(b) of Article IV (Residence). The United States would impose estate tax on the value of the property held by the RRSP or other entity, while Canada would impose income tax on a deemed distribution of the property in the RRSP or other entity. Subparagraph 7(c) provides that for the purpose of paragraph 7 of Article XXIX B, the tax imposed in Canada is imposed in respect of property situated in Canada. This provision ensures that the Canadian income tax will be allowable as a credit against the U.S. estate tax.

Article 27

Article 27 of the Protocol provides the entry into force and effective date of the provisions of the Protocol.

Paragraph 1

Paragraph 1 provides generally that the Protocol is subject to ratification in accordance with the applicable procedures in the United States and Canada. Further, the Contracting States shall notify each other by written notification, through diplomatic channels, when their respective applicable procedures have been satisfied.

Paragraph 2

The first sentence of paragraph 2 generally provides that the Protocol shall enter into force on the date of the later of the notifications referred to in paragraph 1, or January 1, 2008, whichever is later. The relevant date is the date on the second of these notification documents, and not the date on which the second notification is provided to the other Contracting State. The January 1, 2008 date is intended to ensure that the provisions of the Protocol will generally not be effective before that date.

Subparagraph 2(a) provides that the provisions of the Protocol shall have effect in respect of taxes withheld at source, for amounts paid or credited on or after the first day of the second month that begins after the date on which the Protocol enters into force. Further, subparagraph 2(b) provides that the Protocol shall have effect in respect of other taxes, for taxable years that begin after (or, if the later of the notifications referred to in paragraph 1 is dated in 2007, taxable years that begin in and after) the calendar year in which the Protocol enters into force. These provisions are generally consistent with the formulation in the U.S. Model treaty, with the exception that a parenthetical was added in subparagraph 2(b) to address the contingency that the written notifications provided pursuant to paragraph 1 may occur in the 2007 calendar year. Further, subparagraph 3(d) of Article 27 of the Protocol contains special provisions with respect to the taxation of cross-border interest payments that have effect for the first two calendar years that end after the date the Protocol enters into force. Therefore, during this period, cross-border interest payments are not subject to the effective date provisions of subparagraph 2(a).

Paragraph 3

Paragraph 3 sets forth exceptions to the general effective date rules set forth in paragraph 2 of Article 27 of the Protocol.

Dual corporate residence tie-breaker

Subparagraph 3(a) of Article 27 of the Protocol provides that paragraph 1 of Article 2 of the Protocol relating to Article IV (Residence) shall have effect with respect to corporate continuations effected after September 17, 2000. This date corresponds to a press release issued on September 18, 2000 in which the United States and Canada identified certain issues with respect to these transactions and stated their intention to negotiate a protocol that, if approved, would address the issues effective as of the date of the press release.

Certain payments through fiscally transparent entities

Subparagraph 3(b) of Article 27 of the Protocol provides that new paragraph 7 of Article IV (Residence) set forth in paragraph 2 of Article 2 of the Protocol shall have effect as of the first day of the third calendar year that ends after the Protocol enters into force.

Permanent establishment from the provision of services

Subparagraph 3(c) of Article 27 of the Protocol sets forth the effective date for the provisions of Article 3 of the Protocol, pertaining to Article V (Permanent Establishment) of the Convention. The provisions pertaining to Article V shall have effect as of the third taxable year that ends after the Protocol enters into force, but in no event shall it apply to include, in the determination of whether an enterprise is deemed to provide services through a permanent establishment under paragraph 9 of Article V of the Convention, any days of presence, services rendered, or gross active business revenues that occur or arise prior to January 1, 2010. Therefore, the provision will apply beginning no earlier than January 1, 2010 and shall not apply with regard to any presence, services or related revenues that occur or arise prior to that date.

Withholding rates on cross-border interest payments

Subparagraph 3(d) of Article 27 of the Protocol sets forth special effective date rules pertaining to Article 6 of the Protocol relating to Article XI (Interest) of the Convention. Article 6 of the Protocol sets forth a new Article XI of the Convention that provides for exclusive residence State taxation regardless of the relationship between the payer and the beneficial owner of the interest. Subparagraph 3(d), however, phases in the application of paragraph 1 of Article XI during the first two calendar years that end after the date the Protocol enters into force. During that period, paragraph 1 of Article XI of the Convention permits source State taxation of interest if the payer and the beneficial owner are related or deemed to be related by reason of paragraph 2 of Article IX (Related Persons) of the Convention ("related party interest"), and the interest would not otherwise be exempt under the provisions of paragraph 3 of Article XI as it read prior to the Protocol. However, subparagraph 3(d) also provides that the source State taxation on such related party interest is limited to 7 percent in the first calendar year that ends after entry into force of the Protocol and 4 percent in the second calendar year that ends after entry into force of the Protocol.

Subparagraph 3(d) makes clear that the provisions of the Protocol with respect to exclusive residence based taxation of interest when the payer and the beneficial owner are not related or deemed related ("unrelated party interest") applies for interest paid or credited during the first two calendar years that end after entry into force of the Protocol.

The withholding rate reductions for related party interest and exemptions for unrelated party interest will likely apply retroactively. For example, if the Protocol enters into force on June 30, 2008, paragraph 1 of Article XI, as it reads under subparagraph 3(d) of Article 27, will have the following effect during the first two calendar years. First, unrelated party interest that is paid or credited on or after January 1, 2008 will be exempt from taxation in the source State. Second, related party interest paid or credited on or after January 1, 2008 and before January 1, 2009, will be subject to source State taxation but at a rate not to exceed 7 percent of the gross amount of the interest. Third, related party interest paid or credited on or after January 1, 2009 and before January 1, 2010, will be subject to source State taxation but at a rate not to exceed 4 percent of the gross amount of the interest. Finally, all interest paid or credited after January 1, 2010, will be subject to the regular rules of Article XI without regard to subparagraph 3(d) of Article 27.

Further, the provisions of subparagraph 3(d) ensure that even with respect to circumstances where the payer and the beneficial owner are related or deemed related under the provisions of paragraph 2 of Article IX, the source State taxation of such cross-border interest shall be no greater than the taxation of such interest prior to the Protocol.

Gains

Subparagraph 3(e) of Article 27 of the Protocol provides the effective date for paragraphs 2 and 3 of Article 8 of this Protocol, which relate to the changes made to paragraphs 5 and 7 of Article XIII (Gains) of the Convention. The changes set forth in those paragraphs shall have effect with respect to alienations of property that occur (including, for greater certainty, those that are deemed under the law of a Contracting State to occur) after September 17, 2000. This date corresponds to the press release issued on September 18, 2000 which announced the intention of the United States and Canada to negotiate a protocol that, if approved, would incorporate the changes set forth in these paragraphs to coordinate the tax treatment of an emigrant's gains in the United States and Canada.

Arbitration

Subparagraph 3(f) of Article 27 of the Protocol pertains to Article 21 of the Protocol which implements the new arbitration provisions. An arbitration proceeding will generally begin two years after the date on which the competent authorities of the Contracting States began consideration of a case. Subparagraph 3(f), however, makes clear that the arbitration provisions shall apply to cases that are already under consideration by the competent authorities when the Protocol enters into force, and in such cases, for purposes of applying the arbitration provisions, the commencement date shall be the date the Protocol enters into force. Further, the provisions of Article 21 of the Protocol shall be effective for cases that come into consideration by the competent authorities after the date that the Protocol enters into force. In order to avoid the potential for a large number of MAP cases becoming subject to arbitration immediately upon the expiration of two years from entry into force, the competent authorities are encouraged to develop and implement procedures for arbitration by January 1, 2009, and begin scheduling arbitration of otherwise unresolvable MAP cases in inventory (and meeting the agreed criteria) prior to two years from entry into force.

Assistance in collection

Subparagraph 3(g) of Article 27 of the Protocol pertains to the date when the changes set forth in Article 22 of the Protocol, relating to assistance in collection of taxes, shall have effect. Consistent with the third protocol that entered into force on November 9, 1995, and which had effect for requests for assistance on claims finally determined after November 9, 1985, the provisions of Article 22 of the Protocol shall have effect for revenue claims finally determined by an applicant State after November 9, 1985.